bush
PUBLISHING
& associates

Endorsements

"This is not your typical biblical finance book. No matter where you are in your financial walk, God's authority on money in this book will take you to where He wants you to be."

Don Cason
Pastor, Hope Chapel Foursquare Church

"It was awesome to read Ken's book. His book will change and challenge your thoughts about money with biblical and spiritual truths."

Dr. Kwang Jacob Won
Senior Pastor, Charleston Truth Alliance Church

GOD'S PLAN for FINANCIAL VICTORY

Kenton N. Lor

Unless otherwise indicated, all Scripture quotations are taken from the NIV, New International Version, Zondervan Publishing House, 1984, Publishers.

God's Plan for Financial Victory
ISBN: 978-1-944566-62-3

Copyright ©2024 Kenton N. Lor

Bush Publishing & Associates, LLC books may be order at your favorite online bookstore, and everywhere books are sold, including B&N.com.
For further information, please contact:
Bush Publishing & Associates
Tulsa, Oklahoma
www.bushpublishing.com

Disclaimer: This book is intended for informational and educational purposes only. Neither the author nor the publisher is engaged in rendering financial or investment advice. Any investment can become worthless at any time. If financial, investment, or other expert assistance is needed, the services of an appropriately licensed professional should be sought. The author and publisher disclaim any liability that is incurred from the use or application of the contents of this book.

No portion of this book may be used or reproduced by any means: graphic, electronic or mechanical, including photocopying, recording, taping, or by any information storage retrieval system, without the written permission of the publisher, except in the case of brief quotations embodied in critical articles and reviews.

DEDICATIONS

"To my wife, Choua, who has been my most profound inspiration, my biggest supporter, and the driving force that always pushes me to be a better me."

"To my children, Aceline, Faith, Serenity, Brandon, Jacob, and Chloe, who are the joy of my life as well as my strength when I needed most."

ACKNOWLEDGEMENTS

I would like to thank Rev. Pranee Kosolpradit McDonald for her ceaseless support of my spiritual walk with God, her always speaking strength and wisdom into me and my wife, her prayers of blessings over my family and everything that I do, and her reading of my book manuscript and helping to make this publication possible. For this, I am forever thankful.

I am grateful for Craig and Laura McKown for their friendship and openness to share their wisdom in the Word of God with me and my wife, which has helped us as a couple and our family to grow and developed in the faith. Not only that, but I want to thank them both for taking the time to go over the manuscript of my book and Craig for sharing with me his perspective on finance which enabled me to make the subject matter of this book relevant.

I wish to thank Dr. Kwang Jacob Won and his wife, MinKyung Rachel Won, for their reading and support of my book. I greatly appreciate Dr. Won's written comments regarding the biblical aspects of this book. His input has greatly helped me to flesh out the book to ensure its content remains scriptural. Additionally, I want to thank them for their prayers of wisdom and blessings over me and my family. For this, I am very grateful.

To Pastor Don and Carol Cason, thank you so much for being an amazing spiritual father and mother to my family. Since the day my family and I first stepped foot into your church, you both have been so wonderful to us and viewed us as family, not just church members. Also, I want to thank Pastor Don for showing me what humbleness of character looks like as it has helped me to walk in humility. Furthermore, I am grateful for his critical review of my book manuscript and input, which has aided me tremendously in fine tuning this book.

TABLE OF CONTENTS

FOREWORD xiii

INTRODUCTION xv

CHAPTER I: SATAN'S FIGHT AGAINST OUR
    FINANCIAL HEALTH 1

CHAPTER II: UNDERSTANDING THE ENEMY'S TACTICS 15

CHAPTER III: THE ENEMY SEEKS TO SOW CONFUSION 27

CHAPTER IV: THE ENEMY'S MECHANISM OF FINANCIAL
    DECEPTION 41

CHAPTER V: BREAKING THE SPIRITUAL CYCLE
    OF FINANCIAL DECEPTION 57

CHAPTER VI: PREPARING FOR FINANCIAL VICTORY 77

CHAPTER VII: THE TRUTH ABOUT DEBT 99

CHAPTER VIII: KINGDOM PRINCIPLES
    TO INVESTING–PART ONE 115

CHAPTER IX: KINGDOM PRINCIPLES TO
    INVESTING–PART TWO 133

CHAPTER X: KINGDOM PRINCIPLES TO
    INVESTING–PART THREE 153

FOREWORD

I can remember the Friday night following dinner when Ken told me about the book he was writing called "God's Plan for Financial Victory." Instantly he had my attention, as I am very passionate about God's plan for our lives and victory in our finances according to the Word of God! In my opinion, two of the greatest needs we have in the world today is a clear focus on God's plan for our lives and a grasp of biblical stewardship or what I refer to as biblical economics.

I have read a plethora of books and articles on finance, financial stewardship, investing, tithes, offerings, vows and the list goes on and on. However, when I began to read "God's Plan for Financial Victory" I was drawn in by every chapter, paragraph, sentence and word. Ken has this amazing ability, through the anointing of God, to take the complexities of finance and investing strategies and bring them into the realm of simplistic understanding and application.

I believe this is a MUST READ for anyone who is interested in developing a sure foundation, based upon the Word of God, for practical wealth building through investing. You may not believe that you are called to pulpit ministry but one of the greatest privileges that we have as a believer is to play our part in funding the end time harvest of souls. You will never be able to give what you do not have and you will never have until you learn the principles of receiving.

Ken teaches us these principles of receiving through the principles of investing based upon the Word of God. Not only will you receive an abundance of wealth building scripture but you will receive practical steps to achieving your financial goals through investing, which both are instrumental in laying the foundation for the potential of abundant blessings in your life.

I encourage you throughout the next ten chapters to commit yourself as a student to receive the wealth of knowledge and understanding as Ken teaches you investment principles founded upon the Word of God that has the potential to radically change your life to become the financial steward that God has called you to be.

Kevin L. Howell
Lead Pastor, Life Restoration Church

INTRODUCTION

Many believers have heard of the Parable of the Talents. In this story, a master was going away and entrusted his talents and money to three of his servants. Ever wonder why the servant who was given the one talent hid his portion and did not invest it like the other two did? It's because he believed and acted on the lies of the Enemy (whether he realized it or not). John 8:44 tells us that Satan is a *"liar and the father of lies."* So, what were the lies in this situation? The Devil could have whispered the following lies into the ears of the servant given the one talent: (i) Learning how to manage money and invest is hard or too much work, and (ii) the servant could lose the master's money by investing and be in big trouble with him, as he was a hard man.

Is it true that learning how to manage money and invest is difficult or too much work? Or was the lie the Enemy told just a cover-up to keep this servant lazy as pointed out by the master when he said to this servant: *"You wicked, lazy servant!"* (Matthew 25:26)? If learning how to handle one's finances is truly not doable, then the servants given the two and five talents would have also not done it. But they did seek financial knowledge, which was how they were able to each double their talents (Matthew 25:20, 22). This tells us that learning how to manage money and invest is very doable. What about the negative opinion the servant given the one talent said about the master being a hard man (Matthew 25:24)? Could it be true or just an excuse for the one talent servant's fear of losing the talent given to him (had he invested it) as suggested by Mathew 25:25? If the master was truly cruel as stated by this servant, the master would not have rewarded the servant who received the two talents the same as the servant given the five talents. According to Matthew 25:21 and 23, both the two and five-talent servants were given the same reward.

So, what's the truth then? The servant given the one talent was a lazy individual, was scared of putting his one talent to work for fear of losing it, and did not desire a close relationship with the master (that's why he didn't know how fair and just his master truly was).

With his lies, Satan planted thoughts in the mind of the servant given the one talent to keep him from acquiring financial knowledge and wisdom. This was why the master only gave this servant one talent according to his ability–because the master already knew what this servant was capable of. When this servant chose to hide his portion instead of investing it, and when the one talent he had was eventually taken and given to someone else… it all happened because he lacked the knowledge, confidence, and skills to manage the talent given to him.

Once upon a time, I, too, was like the servant given the one talent. I believed and acted on the lies of the Enemy (despite being a born-again Christian and whether I realized it or not). So, what were the lies of the Devil in my situation?

One, investing is very easy; and two, if John Doe can make a lot of money from investing in an initial public offering (IPO) stock, then so can I.

Because I believed his lies that investing was easy, Satan was able to keep me from seeking the right financial knowledge and wisdom. As a result of my financial ignorance, I eventually paid dearly for it when I lost $8,000 investing in an IPO stock many years ago. The loss was so excruciatingly painful to bear–especially because I did not have much money then. I was very angry with myself for several months. To think I could build wealth without getting the right financial knowledge and wisdom was foolish. This is what happens when you row with the Enemy: His lies keep you ignorant.

So, what's the truth? First, I was prideful. Because of my pride, I was foolish and truly ignorant in the matters of finance and investing. So, is investing easy? It can be when a person has the right knowledge and wisdom. And second, most IPO investments will not make money for investors.

Sometime after losing that money, I contemplated how I could have been so foolish. That's when God said to me: "Ken, it's your pride"—which was the truth as I just mentioned. So, what is pride? When we think of the word pride, definitions like "having a high opinion of oneself, being proud of one's accomplishments, or conceitedness" come to mind. But pride is more than these things; pride is about putting our desires above God's desires or His will. At that very moment, my spiritual eyes and ears opened up and I finally understood. In Matthew 13:13 Jesus said, *"Though seeing, they do not see; though hearing, they do not hear or understand."* Though I could see and hear, I did not realize that my pride enabled the Enemy to keep my spiritual eyes and ears closed. Thus, I was foolish and ignorant.

The Lord could not do greatness in my financial life because my pride interfered with His ability to do so. Our God is a God of love; therefore, He will not override us. I lost $8,000 because I was not in God's will (under His protection). What I say here is also true of the servant given the one talent. His laziness and lack of relationship with his master were also a result of pride. Had the one-talent servant relinquished his pride and opened up his spiritual eyes and ears, God would have been able to make him the most successful servant in his master's house!

Once I realized this, I gave up my pride. It was only then that God was able to move me to learn what He needed me to learn about being a great financial steward and for His glory. I now know why the IPO I got into didn't pan out the way I had thought. It's because most IPOs do not make money, and a lot of them do not become profitable for many years. Had my pride not interfered with God's will, I would have known this back then and would not have lost the money that I did. In addition, through my experience as an investor, God revealed to me that few investment products can realistically build wealth for most people (which is something the Enemy doesn't want us to know). I will talk more about this in this book.

Isaiah 1:19 says, *"If you are willing and obedient, you will eat the good things of the land."* I now completely understand why the two servants who invested their talents were so successful. It's because they surrendered their pride and saw things from a spiritual angle. In doing so, God enabled them to become wise in their finances. And because they were willing and obedient, they indeed ate the good things of the land. As for me? Once I let go of my pride, saw things God's way, and became willing and obedient to Him, He recouped the $8,000 that I lost and brought victory to my finances.

This is why I'm writing this book: God desires that every one of us have victory in our finances. But it begins with putting away one's pride and opening up one's spiritual eyes and ears. Having said this, *"I pray that the eyes of your heart be enlightened so that you may know the hope to which he has called you, the riches of his glorious inheritance in his holy people"* (Ephesians 1:18).

CHAPTER I
SATAN'S FIGHT AGAINST OUR FINANCIAL HEALTH

What Is Spiritual Warfare?

As believers, we often hear about a spiritual war going on between God's kingdom of light and Satan's forces of darkness with humanity caught in the crossfire. When we think of spiritual warfare, we tend to think of what we see in the movies: People clashing against evil apparitions in a physical world or some other observable realm. In reality, however, this is not the case at all; our struggle against the evil forces of the supernatural doesn't occur the way it is portrayed in the films.

Although we are spirits, our spirits live in physical bodies. Therefore, we do not do battle in a spiritual realm. Instead, spiritual warfare refers to the fighting between the spirits of light and darkness for the control of our mind, the discerning of the truths from the lies, and the application of the truth to extinguish the evil in our lives. With this said, the mind is the battlefield in which we do spiritual warfare against the evil powers of Satan.

When God made Adam, He did so by forming his body from the dust of the earth and gave him the spirit of life thus bringing forth a living soul (Genesis 2:7). It is the soul that houses our mind (which is the center of our thinking, reasoning, and consciousness); our will (which is our capacity to decide or choose); and our emotion (how we feel about our environment or circumstance). It is the soul (which gives rise to our personality) that makes each of us who we are and unique from one another. Of the soul's three distinct components, the mind is the seat of control. Our mind ultimately dictates the decisions that we make and the emotions that we experience. For instance, when something awful happens in our life, such as the death of a loved one, how we process and interpret that in our mind determines whether we will turn away from God or remain faithful. At the same time, how our mind deals with the difficulties of the situation we are in can influence how we feel, such as being sad, depressed, and/or angry. Our emotions, in turn, can influence our thinking and sway our decision to blame God for our affliction or not.

Because our mind directs our words, actions, and feelings, Satan desires to completely subjugate our mind. If the adversary dominates our mind, he has power and influence over our will and our emotions—hence, our life! So, what does spiritual warfare have to do with our financial health? Everything. The root cause of all our financial problems is spiritual, which I will get into more detail in Chapter IV. All of humanity's problems (regardless of what they are) have a spiritual origin. Satan is an evil spirit; it was he who initially introduced sin into the world (Genesis 3:1-6), which got the ball rolling for all the problems we now have.

The Origin of Spiritual Warfare

The war between light and darkness was brought on by Satan (formerly known as Lucifer) because of his pride and desire to overthrow God from His throne. Although Satan was created by God with great beauty and talents and given much power and authority, he wasn't content. He wanted all of God's power and His kingdom for himself. As a result, Satan went against God. Satan was the first created being of the Lord to have sinful desires and to commit sin.

The Bible defines sin as a transgression against God or His divine laws (1 John 3:4). In other words, to sin means to turn away, disobey, reject, or rebel against God, who is the ultimate and perfect standard for all of existence. Sin isn't just strictly spoken words, an act, or a behavior; a thought can also be a sin (Mark 7:21-23). Sin is always directed against God, no matter who commits it or who the target/receiver of the sin is. For example, in Genesis 4:8, Cain killed his brother Abel. Although Cain committed the sin of murder and Abel was the target of said sin, the sin carried out by Cain was against God (not Abel). Humans are not the only created beings that God's laws apply to; even the angels are subjected to these divine rules. God created the angels to praise, worship, and be in harmony with Him. And this included Satan and his fallen angels as well because they, too, were once angels of light.

So, what truths or laws did Satan initially break? Proverbs 8:13, Proverbs 16:5, James 4:6, and Exodus 20:17 clearly state that God despises pride, arrogance, and covetousness. According to Isaiah 14:13-14 and Ezekiel 28:17, Satan places himself above God, desires God's kingdom, and is very proud of his beauty and qualities. Thus, Satan's nature violated Proverbs 8:13, Proverbs 16:5, James 4:6, and Exodus 20:17. In addition to this, his act of rebellion—which was also a sin (1 Samuel 15:23)—was a complete rejection of God and a transgression against the One who created him in totality.

As a consequence of his rebellion, Satan (along with the angels who turned against God) was cast down from Heaven onto the Earth. In Luke 10:18 Jesus said, *"I saw Satan fall like lightning from Heaven."* Upon realizing that he cannot overpower God and take His kingdom for himself, Satan decided to take revenge by corrupting and destroying mankind beginning with Adam and Eve in the Garden of Eden. Aside from destroying the lives of all people, Satan's ultimate plan is to keep humanity away and eternally separated from God. So the spiritual fight between the forces of light and darkness began in Heaven and came to the Earth after Satan was removed from God's kingdom.

Satan, the great adversary of God and humanity, also goes by many other names as well: the Devil, the Great Dragon, the Adversary, the Evil One, the Enemy, the Accuser, the Great Deceiver, and the Serpent.

No One Is Exempt from the Enemy's Spiritual Warfare

1 John 5:19 makes it very clear that our entire world is under the power of Satan and his evil spirits. The word "world" in

this scripture refers to the way mankind thinks, speaks, and acts, which are completely counter to God's nature. As followers of God, we are not immune to the spiritual manipulations of the Evil One; we can still choose to allow him access to our minds. Also, this isn't just a war involving only Christians as some might be led to think or believe. Even those who do not believe in God are also part of this spiritual conflict whether they want to be or not. In fact, 2 Corinthians 4:4 tells us, *"The god of this age [Satan] has blinded the minds of unbelievers so that they cannot see the light of the gospel that displays the glory of Christ, who is the image of God."* The fact that unbelievers are spiritually blind is evidence that they, too, are in this war.

The Enemy does not discriminate between believers and unbelievers because all were created by God; therefore, all are his enemies. From the moment of our conception, we were all conscripted into Satan's spiritual warfare. No one has any say in the matter. That is why we see brothers against brothers, sisters against sisters, families against families, friends against friends, and nations against nations regardless of what we believe—because all are under the influence of the Serpent. Even the Earth itself is a part of the Devil's fight as he can manipulate the natural phenomena of our planet (i.e., lightning and wind [Job 1:16, 19]) to serve his evil purpose to annihilate and enslave humanity. The only choice we have as a human race in this cosmic struggle is who we are going to align with: God or Satan.

The Serpent hates every one of us to the very core of his being just as much as he hates God. He wants us to experience utter anguish in every area of our life. So Satan will inflict as much pain and destruction as he can in the lives of all people across the globe. As John 10:10 bluntly puts it: *"The thief [Satan] comes only to steal and kill and destroy."*

Every one of us is at ground zero—at the forefront of this war. In addition, the Enemy takes no prisoners. Either we align ourselves with God and use His truths to claim victory in our lives or succumb to the Devil's deceptions and be annihilated physically and spiritually. The choice is ours.

The Enemy's Purpose and Target

Satan does not haphazardly attack humanity in his spiritual fight to dominate the world. He has a purpose and it is threefold:

1. To turn Christians away from God
2. To prevent unbelievers from accepting Jesus Christ as Lord and Savior and receiving the gift of eternal salvation
3. To steal, kill, and destroy (John 10:10) both believers and unbelievers

To fulfill his purpose, as I pointed out earlier, the Serpent's ultimate goal is to firmly control the minds of all people—beginning with individuals.

Why is Satan after individuals? Because he knows very well that individuals are the foundation of humanity, which includes people from every corner of the globe. It is the individuals that give rise to various groups of people, couples, and families, which, together, constitute the many communities of people in the world. Communities that share the same territory, culture, and political ideology comprise a certain society (such as the United States, the United Kingdom, or China). Together, the different societies of the world make up humanity.

Much like the foundation of a house, which holds and stabilizes the house above ground, individuals do the same for humanity as a whole. They can keep mankind in the right with God or cause the human race to stumble and turn away from Him. Thus, by having his hands over the minds of individuals, the Enemy effectively has dominion over the entire world.

Satan Does Not Act Alone

In Psalm 139:7-10 King David said, *"Where can I go from your Spirit? Where can I flee from your presence? If I go up to the heavens, you are there; if I make my bed in the depths, you are there. If I rise on the wings of the dawn, if I settle on the far side of the sea, even there your hand will guide me."* In Jeremiah 23:24 God declared, *"Who can hide in secret places so that I cannot see them? Do I not fill the heaven and the earth?"* And Proverbs 15:3 says, *"The eyes of the Lord are everywhere, keeping watch on the wicked and the good."* These passages tell us that God is omnipresent. In other words, He can be everywhere all at once.

Unlike God, Satan can only be in one place at a time. However, the Serpent does have an army of fallen angels at his disposal to carry out his sinister plan to corrupt and destroy mankind. According to Revelation 12:4 and 7, one-third of the angels created by God took up arms alongside Satan when he sinned against God. Through his devilish underlings, the Serpent exerts his evil influences on the minds of both believers and unbelievers—leading them to commit sins or indulge in activities that satisfy only themselves. We are always under the spiritual assaults or observations of Satan because he is the prince of the air and the god of this world (Ephesians 2:2; 2 Corinthians 4:4). Why is this so? Because upon sinning against God in Genesis 3:6, Adam and Eve relinquished their dominion or control of the world, which God gave to them in Genesis 1:28, to Satan. Nevertheless, the Lord still owns the Earth and everything in it (1 Corinthians 10:26).

Although the vast majority of the spiritual influences and attacks on humanity are carried out by Satan's fallen angels, if he so chooses, the Serpent can interfere in an individual's life directly. How do we know this is possible? There were several instances in the Bible where Satan personally dealt with individuals himself, such as the tempting of Jesus (Matthew 4:1-11), the fall of Adam and Eve (Genesis 3:1-7), the tragedies that befell Job (Job 1:13-19), the counting of Israelite troops by King David (1 Chronicles 21:1-5), and the accusation of Joshua the high priest (Zechariah 3:1-4).

Even though nearly all of the Enemy's biddings are executed by his devilish subordinates, Satan is still ultimately responsible for all spiritual assaults against mankind because he is the mastermind behind spiritual warfare.

The Spiritual Battle for Our Financial Health

As with any war, the spiritual war we are engaged in encompasses many battle fronts. There are numerous spiritual battles going on right now in the areas of drug abuse/addiction, depression, anxiety, extramarital affair, genocide, jealousy, racism, abortion, sexual immorality, and so on where the Enemy and his legions of fallen angels are pitting us against ourselves, each other, and God. One of these very important spiritual battles is the fight for our financial well-being. The Bible contains more than 2,000 scriptures on the management of money, wealth, and possessions. Collectively, these passages are God's financial truths to godly financial living for us while we are on this planet. Thus, there is no doubt that God wants us to be good stewards of the money He entrusted to each of us. Not only that, but the Lord has a plan to help us attain and maintain victory in our finances—which is the focus of this book.

Now, why would Satan be concerned about the financial health of believers? Ecclesiastes 4:12 says, *"Though one may be overpowered, two can defend themselves. A cord of three strands is not quickly broken."* Not only does the Devil hate seeing us live a financially prosperous life, but he knows that financially strong Christians who obey the Word of God pose a significant threat to his plan to dominate and enslave the world.

The Enemy is well aware that money is a necessary tool for God's church to do His will and move His kingdom forward in this fallen world. In Matthew 28:19-20, Jesus gave the Great Commission to his disciples (which include the believers of today as well) when he said, *" . . . Go and make disciples of all nations, baptizing them in the name of the Father and of the Son and of the Holy Spirit, and teaching them to obey everything I have commanded you."* It is not God's desire that anyone should perish (2 Peter 3:9). He wants all people to live godly lives to glorify Him. However, it does cost money to do that which God has called us to do while we are on this planet. Why? We live in a broken world; and, in such a world, nothing is free. For example, a church has to pay for things like rent and utilities. Additionally, it costs money to produce Bibles and put them into the hands of people, and Christians doing missionary work and spreading the Word of God need financial support.

Even the gift of eternal salvation that God provided to us wasn't free. It came at a cost: the shedding of the blood of Jesus Christ on the Cross. So if you've ever received something for free in this fallen world, it's because someone else paid the price for it.

Not only that, but financial hardship or living paycheck to paycheck leads to unnecessary stress of the mind, which can and does cause unhappiness, divorce, family instability, a decline in mental and physical health, suicide, and a believer to drift away from God. As we can see, the health of our finances is tied to virtually every part of our life and can give rise to a multitude of negative consequences causing our walk with God to stumble if it isn't optimal. Money is important. If this wasn't true, the Bible would not have upwards of 2,000 verses on the subject matter, and many of us would not be spending 40 hours or more a week making it.

In addition, an unhealthy financial life is a major distraction to the mind concerning doing the will of God. When we experience financial difficulty, such as living paycheck to paycheck, it prevents us from focusing our full attention on doing the work the Lord has commanded us—and this is exactly what the Devil wants. Many people say, "Money is not the most important thing in the world." I don't disagree with this statement. However, can we honestly say that we will not be negatively affected in any capacity by financial distress or a sudden loss of income? Probably not. In Matthew 8:14-15, Jesus went into Peter's house and healed Peter's mother-in-law of her high fever. Why did He do this? Was it to show the power of God or to impress the people in Peter's house? No! It's because Jesus wanted Peter to be 100% attentive to the work that he would be doing as part of Jesus's earthly ministry—that's how important His work was.

Furthermore, a ministry must know how to manage its financial resources if it hopes to grow as well as avoid investment scams. No church ever grew or stayed strong and did so without properly managing the money at its disposal. Do not think for a second that the Enemy will not try to rob God's church of its money and believers of their life savings. In just the last several decades, many churches and Christians have been defrauded and suffered catastrophic financial losses of billions of dollars as a result of falling for unscrupulous investment products. Some of these churches had to close their doors, and many individual believers lost their entire life savings. Therefore, it is crucial that we, as children of God, have a solid knowledge and understanding of God's financial truths.

Among all the things that Jesus taught, love was the most important. God never meant for the financial wisdom in the Bible to be self-serving. Love isn't just saying good things to people.

It's about doing things that result in benefiting others—even when they can do nothing in return. When we do this, as Christians, we fulfill the requirements of the Great Commandment, which is to love God and to love people (Matthew 22:37-39). So, as children of the Lord Almighty, He wants us to have victory in our finances so that we can be a financial blessing to others. Being a financial blessing to others isn't just about providing them with financial support. It is also about imparting God's financial knowledge and wisdom to them too, so they can have victory in their finances according to the Lord's way and become a financial blessing themselves to even more people as well. And unlike money, knowledge and wisdom can never be used up.

When there is victory in our financial life, according to God's financial principles, this brings harmony to our mind as well as greater joy to our life. Additionally, we will be unhindered and undistracted in our work to bring all people to God and teach them to live according to His truths.

Sadly, there are too many believers struggling financially. Just one Christian or person experiencing financial distress is one too many in God's eyes. However, like a shepherd who goes in search of the one sheep of the hundred that wandered away (Luke 15:3-7), God continuously seeks after the one or those who have gone astray from the financial life that He desires for us to live. God does not want us to neglect our financial health while we are on this planet.

Why are our finances so important to God? Because we are all ambassadors of the King of kings and the kingdom of God. When we go about our daily lives and minister the Word of God to people, we represent the Lord of all creation to the world. This is why He wants us to be successful not only in our financial life but also in every area of life, such as in our thinking, marriages, jobs, health, education, and so on. Our victories are testimonies of how amazing and awesome our God is to all of those whom we come into contact with and who do not know Him.

And so the Serpent's sole purpose in the spiritual battle for our financial health is to keep as many believers as he can in perpetual financial darkness. But Satan was already defeated at the Cross when Jesus took all of our sins upon Himself and said, *"...It is finished"* (John 19:30). Christ's death, resurrection, and ascension showed us that He has already defeated the Enemy by *"...having disarmed the powers and authorities [of Satan and his evil underlings and]... made a public spectacle of them...."* (Colossians 2:15). Additionally, God has given us the power through the Holy Spirit and the knowledge and wisdom of the Bible and in this book to claim victory in the spiritual fight for our financial health.

Isaiah 1:19 says, *"If you are willing and obedient, you will eat the good things of the land [–that is victory in your finances]."*

CHAPTER II
UNDERSTANDING THE ENEMY'S TACTICS

The Effects of Sin

How exactly does Satan rob and destroy us financially? Before we can answer this question, we must first understand the effects of sin as well as the weapons and tactics Satan employs against us. According to Genesis 1:26-27, when God made Adam and Eve, they were pure and sinless in spirit and body because they were made in God's image and likeness. Thus, their nature was pure like that of God. Nevertheless, Adam and Eve did possess the ability to sin because of their free will. How do we know that they had free will? In Genesis 2:16-17 God said, *"You are free to eat from any tree in the garden, but you must not eat from the tree of knowledge of good and evil, for when you eat from it you will certainly die."* This Bible passage tells us God bestowed upon Adam and Eve the gift of free will. It wouldn't make sense for God to give them such a command if they couldn't decide for themselves. Thus, when the Serpent convinced Eve to eat from the Tree of Knowledge of good and evil, she chose to do so and Adam followed suit. As a result, sin entered the world.

Because of their actions (really just Adam's since he is the foundation of mankind and all descended from him [Romans 5:12]), the body and nature (i.e., character, disposition, personality, temperament, and so forth) of man became corrupted. Through that corruption, man seeks to operate in ways that do not conform to God's character, truths, laws, principles, etc. This tendency of man to function opposite of God is called the flesh, which was evidenced by Adam and Eve's self-will, self-centeredness, blaming of others, disloyalty, and disobedience (Genesis 3:6-8, 10-13). The flesh of man is 100% in direct conflict with God's divine nature. That is why Galatians 5:17 tells us, *"...The flesh desires what is contrary to the Spirit [of God], and the Spirit what is contrary to the flesh."* Sin altered the nature of man, giving rise to characteristics that enable ungodly desires to be stirred up and/or harbored within man. Three such characteristics of the flesh that contribute to experiencing difficulty with financial management are pride, foolishness, and ignorance. I will talk more about these as we go forward. In addition, sin conferred upon the body physical flaws like sickness, aging, and death (which were not part of God's original design).

So, why does man have a proclivity for doing that which is opposite to God? Because sin is a spiritual virus that infects and weakens the body and alters human nature in the same way that the human immunodeficiency virus (HIV) destroys the body's immune system. When the body is infected with

HIV it can develop AIDS, a condition that damages white blood cells called helper T-cells, which are part of the body's immune system. When this happens the fighting capabilities of the helper T-cells are diminished and are unable to fight off everyday infections, such as the common cold, which can become life-threatening to the body. Therefore, HIV/AIDS makes the body prone to diseases and illnesses.

Analogous to HIV/AIDS, sin infects, incapacitates, and reprograms the body and the nature of man—giving rise to the flesh, which only yearns for self-satisfaction and darkness over God. Despite our spirit's willingness to seek or follow God, without our mind aligning with it, our spirit can do nothing. Aside from sickness, aging, and physical death, sin also gives rise to other physical deficiencies, such as hunger and exhaustion, thereby weakening the body further.

For example, in Matthew 26:40, when Jesus returned from praying, He found Peter and Zebedee's two sons, John and James, who were supposed to be keeping watch, asleep. To them, Jesus then said, *"The spirit is willing, but the flesh is weak"* (Matthew 26:41). Just a few verses before this, in Matthew 26:35, all the disciples said that they would never turn away from Jesus regardless of what happens, which was the will of their strong spirits. Despite their firm declaration, Peter and the others still succumbed to the weariness of their bodies and fell asleep—which is a weakness of the flesh. But why did they submit to the fatigue of their flesh? Because their minds were ruled by their flesh. And their minds dictated their will to act according to their flesh. This is why Romans 8:7

says, *"The mind governed by the flesh is hostile to God; it does not submit to God's law [way], nor can it do so."*

Since it was Satan who introduced sin to humanity, he knows full well the grip and power sin has on us. That's why in Romans 7:18-20 NLT the Apostle Paul said, *"I want to do what is right, but I can't. I want to do what is good, but I don't. I don't want to do what is wrong [or counter to God], but I do it anyway. But if I do what I don't want to do, I am not the one doing wrong; it is sin living in me that does it."*

Satan's Primary Weapons are Deceptions and Lies

The Serpent is the father of lies just like John 8:44 states: *"He [Satan] was a murderer from the beginning, not holding to the truth, for there is no truth in him. When he lies, he speaks his native language, for he is a liar and the father of lies."* Therefore, in every spiritual battle, including the one for our financial health, the Enemy's tools for bringing havoc on man are deceptions and lies. Here, deception is the act of convincing a person's mind that a lie is true so that they might think, speak, and/or act contrary to God. The lies of the Devil come in many different forms, but the most recognized is spoken words. Nevertheless, other ways he can present his lies are written words, images, songs, whispers, drugs, persons (men and women), places, things, voices, and so on. Since God is truth (John 14:6), anything contrary to Him is a lie. Genesis 3:1 tells us that Satan is quite clever in his deceptive dealings. Thus, he will use whatever he can to deceive us.

The fall of Adam and Eve from paradise is a prime example of Satan's lies in action and marks the beginning of his spiritual warfare against mankind. The Serpent initiated his deception by first tripping up Eve when he said to her: *"Did God really say, 'You must not eat from any tree in the garden'?"* (Genesis 3:1). In response, Eve said that she and Adam could eat from any tree, except for the Tree of Knowledge because they would die if they ate from it. Upon hearing this, Satan told Eve two lies to arouse her to eat from that tree: First, *"You will not certainly die..."* (Genesis 3:4) and second, *"For God knows that when you eat from it your eyes will be opened, and you will be like God [gain Deity status], knowing good and evil"* (Genesis 3:5). Here, the Enemy's lies are in the form of spoken words. Eve was immediately convinced by the Enemy's lies because they sounded wonderful. As a result, she ate from the Tree of Knowledge and gave some of its fruit to Adam and he, too, ate.

When it comes to our financial life, Satan also deceives us in much the same way he beguiled Adam and Eve. For instance, the Serpent may convince us that penny stocks, which are stocks that trade for less than $1 with a market capitalization of often less than $250 million, are great to invest in as they are incredibly cheap and will make us rich once their prices surge. On the surface, this seems to be true; but we find out that it is a lie when we dig deeper. Many times, this kind of lie will come to people in the form of online articles and YouTube videos on penny stock investing. The incredibly low prices of penny stocks and the potential to make big gains fast are what draw investors to them. For example, DEF penny stock trading for $0.50 can jump to $2 in a matter of a month based on really good news surrounding the stock or pure investor hype. Thus, a $10,000 position in the stock would become = ($10,000/$0.50) x $2 = $40,000 (which is a rise of 400%).

Although it is possible to make a lot of money from owning penny stocks, the reality is that the chance of doing so is incredibly low. Why? Because more than 99% of penny stocks do not thrive. In other words, the companies of these stocks do not make money or become profitable. Therefore, the vast majority of people who pour their money into these investments will either lose their money or gain little to nothing.

Here's what God has to say about trying to make a lot of money fast in penny stocks (or anything of this nature): *"Wealth gained hastily will dwindle..."* (Proverbs 13:11 ESV). In other words, the $0.50 DEF penny stock, which has the potential to quickly skyrocket, could instead very easily decline in value to $0.10 in just a few days based on some bad news or investor fears, which equates to an 80% drop. In this situation, a $10,000 investment in the stock would dwindle to $2,000. In fact, according to historical performances of penny stocks, a downside scenario is more likely than a sustained upside story.

There are well over 10,000 penny stocks. Some of these were once stocks of companies that did very well financially or were highly favored by investors but fell from grace. So, which of these penny stocks will become successful or successful again? No one knows (except for God). Therefore, investing in penny stocks is very much like buying lottery tickets or gambling at a casino.

The Enemy's Methods to Rob and Destroy Us Financially

Spiritual influence and spiritual attack are the two methods of spiritual assault the Devil uses to get us to:
- Fall into financial hardship
- Live paycheck to paycheck
- Do nothing to improve our financial situation
- Outright reject God

Both deceptions and lies are at the heart of these two tactics. Here's an example of spiritual influence in action: Let's say Ahaziah has been very blessed by God and makes $100,000 a year. He is out shopping for an SUV and is contemplating whether to buy a new or used one. The Enemy's lies seep into Ahaziah's mind and persuade him to buy a new $60,000 SUV instead of a $25,000 used one. The Devil tells him that such a ride will be more fitting of his financial stature and more reliable. In addition, the Enemy tells Ahaziah just how amazing and cool he will look in his new SUV. Here, the lies are images going through Ahaziah's mind of an awesome-looking new SUV and his friends all giving him thumbs-up.

But the truth is whether an automobile is new or used has nothing to do with its reliability. Assuming there is no manufacturing defects or problems with the vehicle, how Ahaziah drives and maintains the SUV will play a greater role in the car's reliability. Because we do live in a fallen world, Ahaziah can lose his six-figure salary job at any time and for any reason. Unless Ahaziah is already very financially healthy, he will feel the financial pain from his expensive SUV immediately upon being let go from his high-paying job—

which won't be so amazing and is exactly what Satan wants him to feel. In addition, as with anything, the excitement that comes with the new SUV will eventually fade.

On the other hand, in a spiritual attack, the Devil uses force to get our mind to outright reject God. So Ahaziah goes to work one day and finds out that his company has decided to slash 50% of its workforce. Unfortunately, his $100,000 job (which Ahaziah has been in for about three years) is one of those being eliminated in two weeks. Once the job goes away, all employment benefits, including healthcare coverage, also cease. Ahaziah only has $1,000 in his savings account and a $300,000 mortgage; $40,000 in student loans; and that $60,000 SUV—all of which Ahaziah will soon no longer be able to make the payments for. Because of the financial bind Ahaziah is in, he will most likely lose his home and vehicle and possibly default on his student loan debt. Furthermore, Ahaziah has two small children and a spouse to feed and support. To make matters worse, he is having a difficult time finding work, and jobs that offer a similar salary to his current position are far and few between. With only two days before his job goes away, stress, anxiety, anger, and frustration all kick into high gear. Because of what is happening to him, Ahaziah blames God for his difficult circumstance and stops attending church as well as his weekly Bible study.

As I said, we live in a fallen world and what I described above can and does happen all the time, and Satan uses it to turn Christians away from God. How? Because the flesh desires someone to blame to be satisfied. That was exactly what Adam and Eve did after eating from the Tree of Knowledge:

Adam blamed Eve for his error, and Eve faulted the Serpent for misleading her. If we think about it, doesn't the above scenario sound familiar? It should. Does the story of Job ring a bell? Job was subjected to Satan's spiritual attacks. And for what? To get Job to curse God, of course. All of Job's oxen, donkeys, and camels were taken from him by the Sabeans (Job 1:15) and Chaldeans (Job 1:17), and many of his servants were killed by these people. Then, Job's children, servants, and sheep were killed by natural disasters that seemingly appeared by chance (Job 1:16, 19).

In many cases of employment losses, the cause is due to financial mismanagement at the top. When a company loses money, shedding employees from the payroll is typically the result. And it is safe to say that the minds of some of the folks (if not all), who control the company and its finances were spiritually influenced by Satan, which led to financial decisions that were contrary to God's money principles that eventually triggered the layoff of workers.

Do we think it was just a coincidence that both the Sabeans and the Chaldeans happened to plunder Job? Of course not. As readers seeing things "from the outside in," we know it was the Devil who was responsible for the calamities in Job's life. The minds of these two groups of people were spiritually controlled by Satan behind the scenes such that it led them to attack and kill Job's servants and take his animals. However, a person who is in a similar situation as Ahaziah sees things "from the inside out." Thus, it would be difficult for them to see that it was the evil influences of the Enemy that led or contributed to their layoff and the mishandling of their own finances.

The Enemy fears Christians who obey the Word, which includes God's financial truths because they are a threat to his rulership and control of the Earth. That is why he will do whatever is necessary to prevent believers from becoming financially healthy or to sway followers of God to turn away from the truth.

The Enemy is Subtle in His Spiritual Assaults

One of the main reasons why many people, including some Christians, find it difficult to believe that spiritual warfare is going on behind the scenes is due to the incredibly subtle nature of Satan's spiritual influence and attack. For example, in Job 1:16 and 19, the Bible tells us how Job's sheep, some servants, and children were killed. His sheep and servants were struck down by fire falling from the sky, and his sons and daughters died as a result of a strong wind causing the eldest son's house to collapse on them. To many, they see Job's tragic losses as the results of unexpected or unforeseen acts of nature—nothing more and nothing less. After all, people do get killed by natural disasters all the time. And rarely, if ever, do the news agencies report them as acts of or associating with the supernatural. Thus, we just pass them off as natural disaster-related accidents.

In Matthew 16:21-23, Jesus told His disciples about His plan to go to Jerusalem where He would suffer, be killed, and rise again. Immediately upon hearing this, Peter took Jesus aside and said that he wouldn't allow any of these things to happen to Him. However, Peter had no idea the words he had just spoken were in conflict with God's plan for mankind's redemption and salvation and that those words had been planted in his mind by Satan to thwart God's work. But in verse 23, it was revealed by Jesus that Satan was the culprit behind Peter's thoughts. Most believers would have responded the same way as Peter did and never realized that it was the Enemy who was pulling the strings from behind the curtain.

Satan is the Great Deceiver. His interventions in every facet of our lives are carefully orchestrated so that they appear as if they occur naturally or by random chance. The Serpent wants us to believe that our enemy is flesh and blood. He is so good at convincing us of this, which is why we quarrel among ourselves and blame each other for the problems we have. The idea of the Enemy is to blind us from the real source of all our problems: Satan himself. When we don't know the true source of our financial problems, we treat only the symptoms. This is why so many Christians continue to experience financial difficulties like financial hardship, living paycheck to paycheck, and debt overload.

The Bible explicitly tells us that "*...our struggle is not against flesh and blood, but against the rulers, against the authorities, against the powers of this dark world and against the spiritual forces of evil in the heavenly realms*" (Ephesians 6:12). It's pretty clear that spiritual warfare is real, and our true adversary is Satan (not people).

CHAPTER III
THE ENEMY SEEKS TO SOW CONFUSION

Why Are Some Believers Unsure of Financial Prosperity in Their Walk with God?

There are many Christians who are confused about where God stands when it comes to financial prosperity. That's because the Enemy uses deceptions and lies to distort the Word of God to sow confusion into the minds of believers. Two such lies that he wants Christians to believe are:

- The Bible teaches a message that believers ought to be poor to truly serve the Lord righteously.
- Any focus on money might draw Christians away from God or give others the impression that followers of the Lord are only financially driven.

Of course, both of these notions are false. But the Enemy's aim is to get believers to pay little to no attention to their finances until it's too late. Satan knows that money is a necessary tool to do God's work on this planet, and it is essential to our overall health. That's why he wants to keep as many believers as he can in perpetual financial darkness. Hence, when we buy into his lies, we are only helping the Devil fulfill his purpose.

For example, in Matthew 6:19-20, Jesus said, *"Do not store up for yourselves treasures on earth, where moths and vermin destroy, and where thieves break in and steal. But store up for yourselves treasures in heaven, where moths and vermin do not destroy, and where thieves do not break in and steal."* Because of this passage, some believers are led by Satan to believe that financial prosperity on Earth is unbiblical. However, if we examine verse 21 of Matthew 6, which says, *"For where your treasure is, there your heart will be also,"* along with verses 19 and 20, we will see that God was referring to the alignment of our heart—is it with God or something else?

Many Bible verses appear to conflict with themselves or other passages. However, the truth is God does not and cannot contradict Himself. If we find ourselves contemplating on the contradictory nature of scriptures, it's because Satan wants us to turn the other way and be defeated.

In addition to the Devil twisting the truths of the Bible, God's authority on money is rarely taught in the church. Also, many Christian schools do not educate or train students to have a clear understanding of God's position on financial prosperity as well as their role in being a good financial steward in the Lord's kingdom (i.e., how being a good manager of money according to the Word is important to effectively carry out the Great Commission given to us by Jesus and to one's well-being). Furthermore, some Bible studies programs do not offer students a course in biblical finance at all. For these reasons, some followers are not sure about financial prosperity in their walk with God and many continue to struggle financially.

Although money can be a very sensitive and emotional subject to talk about, it needs to be regularly taught in the church as well as in Christian academic settings so that believers can know God's financial truths and His position on financial prosperity. The Devil wants to keep God's church and school system quiet on this very important subject matter because he knows that Christians who know the truth are very dangerous and are a great threat to him.

Is God Against Financial Prosperity?

3 John 2 says, *"Dear friend, I pray that you may enjoy good health and that all may go well with you, even as your soul is getting along well."* Based on this scripture, God desires that believers prosper not only in their health and spirits but also in their finances as well. How do we know this? Financial wellness is included in the part that says, *"that all may go well with you."* However, Satan will try to tell us that 3 John 2 has nothing to do with God wishing for believers to be in good financial health and that it was just a letter written by the Apostle John to his friend Gaius wishing him well in general—that's all.

But I do not believe that John would write such a greeting and not want his friend to truly be well in every area of his life, including his finances. In John 15:14-15, Jesus called His disciples His friends. Thus, as Christians, we are not only sons and daughters of God; we are also His friends. Additionally,

2 Timothy 3:16 tells us, *"All Scripture is God-breathed... "*; therefore, 3 John 2 is God speaking to us directly Himself and wishing that we, His friends, be well in our health, spirits, finances, and other areas of life. As believers, we need to know our position in God. When we don't know who we are or our position in God, the Serpent can trick us into believing that we can't be this or have that.

In addition, during biblical times, many believers were extremely well off. Genesis 13:2 tells us that Abraham *"... had become very wealthy in livestock and in silver and gold."* Further, in verse 6 of Genesis 13, we are told that Abraham and his nephew, Lot, could no longer stay together because of the massive possessions between just the two of them. According to Job 1:3 it says, *"...He [Job] owned seven thousand sheep, three thousand camels, five hundred yokes of oxen, and five hundred donkeys, and had a large number of servants."* King David was quite blessed with massive wealth himself. After defeating the army of Hadadezer, King David was given many things made of gold, silver, and bronze from King Tou of Hamath (2 Samuel 8:9-10). From 1 Chronicles 29:4, we are then told that King David had *"three thousand talents of gold... and seven thousand talents of refined silver...,"* which he gave for the building of God's temple. In every single one of these cases, it was God Himself who blessed and enabled the believer to acquire such wealth and possessions. God does not prohibit Christians from becoming financially prosperous.

If God doesn't desire that we be financially prosperous in any capacity, why would He put so much good financial knowledge and wisdom in the Bible? After all, there are more than 2,000 scriptures that deal with money directly or indirectly. Additionally, aside from the subject of sin, money and possession are the other two topics most referenced in the Bible. It doesn't make any sense for God to waste so many pages of the Bible to include knowledge and wisdom He doesn't want us to use. In truth, our God is not a wasteful God. According to John 6:12, *"When they had all had enough to eat, he [Jesus] said to his disciples, 'Gather the pieces that are left over. Let nothing be wasted.'"*

Is Money Evil or Sinful?

The Enemy wants Christians to believe that money is not good by feeding our minds with lies. Most of us work to make a living; so, money can't possibly be a bad thing, right? Or is it? To know for sure if money is evil or sinful, we need to examine money with respect to the Word of God's definition of sin. According to 1 John 3:4, sin refers to the violation of God's law, which includes His nature, truths, and principles. To be able to commit sin requires that a person or thing must have free will or the ability to make choices as implied by Genesis 2:16-17. Thus, based on the criteria given by the Bible, money in and of itself is not evil or sinful because it does not possess the free will to break God's law.

However, money can be involved in or used to commit sins by a person who can choose to not conform to God's standard. For instance, 1 Timothy 6:10 warns us that *"...the love of money is a root of all kinds of evil."* According to this scripture, it is not money but the *"love of money"* that is wicked. For example, Judges 16:4-21 gives us the account of Delilah, a woman who loved money. Because of her *"love of money,"* the five rulers of the Philistines were able to get Delilah to trick Samson, who was in love with her, into revealing the secret to his supernatural strength (which was his long hair) for a total of 5,500 shekels of silver. So, what were the "money sins" of Delilah?

- Idolatry—she worshiped money and not God.
- Pride—she put her interest above God's and others'.
- Lying—she told Samson that he doesn't love her to get him to divulge his secret, but Judges 16:4 and 15 indicate that Samson did love Delilah.

So, how much was Samson sold out for? A shekel is about 11 grams; thus, the shekels of silver Delilah received equates to = 5,500 x 11 = 60,500 grams or 2,134 ounces of silver. As of early December 2023, the price of silver was about $25 per ounce. Based on these numbers, Delilah was paid = $25 x 2,134 = $53,350 to betray Samson.

Money itself is not evil or sinful. Money is nothing more than just a tool. It is a person's love of money that is wicked.

Was Jesus Poor or Rich?

According to Luke 2:7, Jesus was born in a manger. Mark 6:3 tells us that the people of His town, Nazareth, said Jesus was just a carpenter. The Devil will use scriptures such as these to deceive us into believing that Jesus was Himself very poor. Thus, we should be poor too. Of course, as with any line of scripture, it is important to also examine passages before and after the verse in question as well as other scriptures to get a complete picture of what is going on.

It isn't necessary to comb through every line of scriptures in the synoptic gospels to explain if Jesus or His earthly ministry had an abundance of money. Whether Christ was rich or not can be decided by two Bible verses. John 1:3 says, *"Through him [Jesus] all things were made; without him, nothing was made that has been made"* and Psalm 24:1-2 tells us, *"The earth is the Lord's, and everything in it, the world, and all who live in it; for he founded it on the seas and established it on the waters."* Based on just these two scriptures alone, there is no question about Jesus's wealth or richness. It's crystal clear that Christ wasn't poor since He is the Creator and Owner of everything to begin with.

But some might say, "If Jesus was rich why did He borrow a colt in Mark 11:1-3?" The purpose of Christ coming to Earth as a "man" was to fulfill God's plan, which was to save and redeem mankind from sin. To do this, Jesus had to become like one of us. As a man, He gave up everything—His richness and glory—for us, including His ownership of the things in people's possession on Earth. That is why in the Gospels of Matthew, Mark, Luke, and John, we never see a scripture where Jesus says to another person: "That thing you own or have belongs to me." According to Mark 11:3, the colt that Jesus borrowed did eventually get returned because it wasn't His. So it's not that Jesus wasn't rich; He just gave it up for our sake. That is why the Bible tells us in 2 Corinthians 8:9 *"...that though he [Jesus] was rich, yet for [our] sake he became poor so that [we] through his poverty might become rich [not just financially but in every area of life]."*

Where Is Our Heart?

We now know that God is not against financial prosperity. In addition, we also know that money itself is not evil or sinful. If this is the case, what then seems to be the problem when it comes to money or financial prosperity? The heart. God is only concerned about our heart: Where is it? With God or money? And this is really where Satan will try to stir up confusion. But first, what is meant by "heart"? Is it the organ inside the body that pumps blood? No. Matthew 9:4 says, *"Knowing their thoughts, Jesus said, 'Why do you entertain evil thoughts in your hearts?;'"* Genesis 6:5 states, *"The Lord saw ... that every inclination of the thoughts of the human heart was only evil all the time;"* and Matthew 15:19 tells us, *"For out of the heart come evil thoughts—murder, adultery, sexual immorality, theft, false testimony, slander."* According to these verses, when the Bible talks about the "heart" it is referring to our "mind" because that's where thoughts are formed. Thus, heart and mind are often used interchangeably in the Bible and Christian writings.

Now, this is where things can get tricky: According to Matthew 6:24 it says, *"No one can serve two masters. Either you will hate the one and love the other, or you will be devoted to one and despise the other. You cannot serve both God and money."* If we are not careful here, Satan will lead us to believe that we cannot possibly live a financially prosperous life while serving the Lord at the same time because that's what this passage seems to suggest. The Evil One will point to the young rich ruler in Matthew 19:16-22 as evidence of this by saying that "because the man had great wealth, he could not truly serve the Lord and decided to not follow Jesus."

However, what we need to understand is that God isn't looking for us to be perfect. Since we are all sinners from conception because of what Adam and Eve did, we can't serve God without stumbling. Regardless of whether we are rich or poor, we are still sinners capable of evil things. For instance, Cain, who had no money, murdered his brother Abel. And King David, who was incredibly financially wealthy, committed adultery by sleeping with Uriah's wife, Bathsheba. Both the rich and the poor can and do commit sins. Romans 3:10 reminds us that no one is righteous. After all, Jesus didn't come to die for only the rich but also the poor—*"for all have sinned..."* (Romans 3:23). Instead, the Lord is most interested in our faith in Him while we pursue financial success or when we are financially well off. That is why Hebrews 11:6 says, *"...without faith, it is impossible to please God...."*

Enoch, who was one of the most blameless human beings to have ever lived and was simply taken up to Heaven by God without experiencing physical death, was still a sinner and not perfect. But it was Enoch's 300 years of incredible faith in his walk with God that won him high praise. Enoch's faith indicated that his heart was also firmly with God. And this is really what God is looking for in all of us. When our faith is in God, our hearts is also with Him. Hence, we will be able to serve God regardless of our financial standings.

Nevertheless, Satan will come at us with every lie in his book of deception to get us to believe that being financially healthy or prosperous won't allow our hearts to line up with

God. He will continue to distort Matthew 6:24 as well as other scriptures to create doubts in our minds that it is not possible to be financially prosperous and still serve only God. Unfortunately for the Devil, God has already shown us that it is possible to serve only Him despite money being in the equation. We only need to look at the story of Abraham to know this.

Abraham wasn't born into wealth but gained his richness along the way (Genesis 12:5, 16; 13:2; 20:14, 16). Yet, because he had faith in God from the beginning, Abraham's great wealth never became a stumbling block to his servanthood to God. Nowhere in the Scripture will we find that Abraham put his wealth ahead of God. Abraham proved to himself and us that his faith and heart were in God (not money) when he willingly sacrificed his only son Isaac (who was his treasure) as a burnt offering to the Lord. With the kind of wealth Abraham had, he could have easily relied on his wealth to circumvent what God asked him to do–but he didn't. How do we know Abraham wasn't reluctant to give up his son? In Genesis 22:16-17 the angel of the Lord told Abraham what God said: *"...because you have... not withheld your son, your only son, I will surely bless you and make your descendants as numerous as the stars in the sky and as the sand on the seashore."*

Of course, God did stop Abraham from actually sacrificing Isaac. We know that God was only testing Abraham and never truly desired for him to sacrifice Isaac as a burnt offering to the Lord because in Deuteronomy 18:10 God said, *"Let no one be found among you [the Israelites] who sacrifices their son or daughter in the fire...."* Additionally, in Jeremiah 19:5, the Lord echoed that child sacrifice in the fire was never something that was in his mind.

Matthew 6:21 tells us, *"For where your treasure is, there your heart will be also."* The word "treasure" in this verse can refer to a lot of things depending on what we consider treasures. It can be our children, money, time, labor, and so on. Unlike with Abraham, God will never ask us to offer up our children as sacrifices to show that our hearts are with God because of what Christ did on the Cross. The work of Jesus completely did away with the entire sacrificial system as He was the perfect sacrifice for all of us. There are other ways that we can demonstrate whether our hearts are with the Lord or money. One such way is tithing, which is the practice of giving a tenth of one's income to their church.

Under the Old Covenant, tithing was required of the Israelites by the laws that were given by God. Of course, the practice of tithing precedes the law. We know this because Abraham gave a tenth of his plunder to Melchizedek in Genesis 14:20 (after rescuing his nephew Lot and defeating Kedorlaomer and his allies). Although the New Covenant under Christ does not require or command followers to tithe, it did not abolish the practice of doing so either. Instead, the New Covenant encourages generous and joyful giving. 2 Corinthians 9:6-7 tells us, *"Whoever sows sparingly will also reap sparingly, and whoever sows generously will also reap generously. Each of you should give what you have decided in your heart to give, not reluctantly or under compulsion, for God loves a cheerful giver."* Although tithing is not required in the New Covenant, as Christians, we should still tithe and do so consistently and unreluctantly. When we do this, it demonstrates that our faith and hearts are in the Lord.

As for the young rich ruler in Matthew 19:16-22, Jesus was just simply testing where his heart truly was—with God or his wealth (in the same way God was testing Abraham)—when He told the man: *"If you want to be perfect, go, sell your possessions and give to the poor, and you will have treasure in heaven. Then come, follow me."* The man thought he was good enough to get eternal life because he claimed to have kept all the commandments Jesus recited in verses 18 and 19. Since the rich man could not give up his possessions to help the poor as Jesus instructed him, he ironically was already violating the commandment to *"...love your neighbor as yourself"*—which was one of the commandments Jesus mentioned in verse 19. Based on his unwillingness and disobedience here, this brings into question whether the young rich ruler upheld the other commandments as he had claimed. Had the young man acted exactly as Jesus told him, God would have stopped him from doing so just as He stopped Abraham from actually sacrificing Isaac because the man's heart (like Abraham's) was truly with God, not his wealth.

The Enemy Wants Us to Believe that Financial Victory Is Too Hard to Achieve

God loves us more than we'll ever know and He wants the very best for us, including our finances. That's why in John 10:10 Jesus said, *"I have come that they [all believers] may have life, and have it to the full."* Financial success and prosperity are included in the *"full"* part of this statement as well.

Otherwise, a believer cannot *"have life, and have it to the full."* In light of everything said thus far, there is no doubt that the Lord wants us to prosper financially. Despite this truth, Satan continues to convince many Christians to believe that cutting costs, increasing their income, saving, and/or investing is too hard to do.

Remember the story of Gideon, the son of Joash the Abiezrite? God told Gideon to go and save His people, the Israelites, from the hands of the Midianites, who had been oppressing them. But Gideon said to God: *"...How can I save Israel? My clan is the weakest in Manasseh, and I am the least in my family"* (Judges 6:15). These spoken words of Gideon, which are lies, were planted in his mind by Satan. The Enemy wanted Gideon to believe that he was incapable of doing what God instructed him. Yet, in Judges 6:12, God called Gideon a mighty warrior, which was before he made the debasing statement about his clan and himself. Why? Because Gideon was who God said he was—a mighty warrior, not who the Enemy said he was—the least.

When God called on Gideon to save the Israelites, he had two choices: either believe the lies of Satan that his clan was the weakest and that he was the least and do nothing, or believe what God said about him and that God would be with him and fight. When it comes to believing, thinking, speaking, and acting there are only two sources that influence these things: God and Satan. We have to decide which source we will align with. Gideon, nonetheless, chose to align with the Lord and believe that he had already won even though he had yet to see victory. How do we know Gideon did have faith in God?

Hebrews 11:32 mentioned Gideon as being among those who were faithful.

So Gideon and 300 Israelite men went to fight the 135,000-troop-strong Midianite army. Even though the odds were up against him, Gideon believed and obeyed the Lord's commands and advanced his troops. As such, God did the impossible for him: The Lord delivered the Midianites into Gideon's hands and gave him victory. Gideon thought he was just a nobody, but look what Gideon accomplished when he believed in God. He was able to free the Israelites from the hands of the Midianites—something he thought was too hard or impossible.

Here's what I want all believers of the One True God to know: In Hebrews 12:2 KJV the Bible tells us, "...*Jesus [is] the author and finisher of our faith.*" Since He is the author and finisher of our faith (not Satan), the Lord knows our future and already sees us at the finish line—financially victorious! When Gideon chose to believe in God, he became an unstoppable force that not even Satan was able to stop with 135,000 enemy soldiers. The Serpent tried to deceive Gideon into believing that he was a nobody but failed miserably. Now he's trying to get us to believe that cutting our costs, increasing our income, saving our money, and/or investing is too hard to do. However, in Matthew 19:26 Jesus said, "*With man this is impossible, but with God all things [including victory in our finances] are possible.*" So, who are we going to believe: God or Satan?

CHAPTER IV
THE ENEMY'S MECHANISM OF FINANCIAL DECEPTION

The Lies Are More Appealing than the Truths

Before a person can break free from the financial darkness the Evil One has bound them to, they must first understand how he deceives them. Eve's disobedience of God's commandment in Genesis 2:17 regarding the Tree of Knowledge provides us with insight as to why we experience financial difficulty. Recall that the Enemy's weapons of choice in spiritual warfare are deceptions and lies. His goal is to influence our mind with his lies to get us to think, speak, and/or act counter to God. When Eve was being deceived by the Serpent to eat from the Tree of Knowledge, she said in Genesis 3:3 that God forbade her and Adam from eating from that tree. If they did eat from it, the pair would certainly die. Yet, after the Devil countered her by saying that she and Adam would not die and would instead become like God (Genesis 3:4-5), Eve reversed her position concerning the tree and ate from it. In her mind, the Serpent's lies were more attractive than

God's truth. It sounded like God was holding out on Adam and Eve and what the Enemy said could be the real truth. So she ate from the Tree of Knowledge and so did Adam, which brought forth death just as God said it would. In addition, neither Adam nor Eve ever became "like God" in the sense that Eve might have thought of it.

Let's take cryptocurrency, also known as crypto, as an investment example. The media for the past several years (as of this writing) has been touting crypto as the wave of the future. It is believed that all global financial transactions will eventually be going virtual with crypto appearing to lead the way. Not only that, but the technology behind crypto (blockchain) can be used for protecting, storing, accessing, and transferring data in a wide variety of settings, such as government, healthcare, retail, and banking. All of this makes crypto very promising and an investment to be in to make millions, which sounds very amazing and enticing. Because of the media frenzy over crypto, everyone wants a piece of this asset class. However, this is exactly what Satan wants us to believe. After all, it was he who planted those thoughts of lies into the minds of the folks running the media.

Now, here's what God tells us about things like crypto: *"Those who work their land will have abundant food, but those who chase fantasies will have their fill of poverty"* (Proverbs 28:19), and *"Wealth gained hastily will dwindle..."* (Proverbs 13:11 ESV). At a glance, these two scriptures sound like God wants us to just work hard, stop chasing our dreams, and doesn't want us to make a lot of money. But here's why God gave us these two wise sayings: Unlike stocks, which are backed by the profits generated from the products and/or services of the companies who issued them, all crypto coins are based largely on investor sentiment. In other words, the values of stocks are supported by and derived from the works of their respective companies, while the worth of all crypto coins is based on investor belief of what is going to happen.

Other things being equal, the U.S. stock market as a whole typically does well over the long term (move upwards gradually) when companies continually make money. Crypto, on the other hand, will climb if investors think or feel great about the crypto market; the opposite is true if investors don't believe or feel much love for these digital assets. But here's the danger: There's no way of knowing how investors will view the crypto market in the short or long term. It's all just a guessing game—even for the crypto experts.

Similar to penny stocks, cryptos have the potential to make a lot of money fast due to surges in their prices. A jump of 10,000% in a short period is not unheard of for cryptos. Nevertheless, the chance of anyone snatching up this kind of gain is very low. There's no way to know when it will occur and which virtual coin or coins out of the thousands in circulation will experience such a climb. Additionally, there is no guarantee that such a price jump will happen. Moreover, cryptos can also tank very rapidly by as much as 70% or more in just a few days without warning. If Elah had $100,000 parked in a digital currency that suffered this kind of loss, it would be a complete nightmare for him.

Like Eve, many people would shun the truths for the lies. Why is this so? Because the lies are more appealing to the mind than the truths as described. Thus, the mind would rather believe the lies over the truths. Although God's truths may not be to our liking, they are there for a reason: to protect us. Had Adam and Eve obeyed the truth (God's command in Genesis 2:17), they would have been protected against Satan's deceptive scheme, and they would still be living the good life. To the Evil One, it doesn't matter whether a person believes his lies or not. His only goal, of course, is to get the person to act on the lies.

The Mind Is Ruled by the Flesh

Our financial problems can also be explained by the fall of Adam and Eve if we dig deeper into why they sinned against God. Recall that the mind is the battlefield of spiritual warfare as it is the control center that dictates the will and emotional aspects of the human soul. Because of sin, the body and human nature have been corrupted and crave that which is counter to God in every conceivable way. This inclination is known as the flesh. In Genesis 2:16-17, God explicitly said to Adam (which also included Eve): *"You are free to eat from any tree in the garden, but you must not eat from the tree of knowledge of good and evil, for when you eat from it you will certainly die."* Despite this divine decree, Adam and Eve still broke God's command. But why did they go against the Lord?

Immediately after Satan lied to Eve in Genesis 3:4-5, the Bible tells us, *"...The woman saw that the fruit of the tree was good for food and pleasing to the eye, and also desirable for gaining wisdom . . . ."* (Genesis 3:6). This was the lust that the Enemy stirred up in Eve for the forbidden fruit before she made the conscious choice to eat from that tree. Thus, Eve sinned against God because her mind (which thought about these things because of the Devil's lies) was controlled by her flesh, which yearned for the fruit of the Tree of Knowledge. In this way, Eve acted through her will according to the desires of her flesh. Hence, the flesh is an ally of the Evil One because it harbors desires that not only contradict God's nature but align with the Enemy. In the case of Eve, she lusts for the fruit of the Tree of Knowledge in the same way that Satan lusts for God's throne and His kingdom. Eve could eat from any tree in the garden except for the Tree of Knowledge. Still, that wasn't enough for her.

Now what about Adam? Satan never spoke a single word to Adam during his entire deceptive ploy against the pair. Nor was Adam even the target of the Serpent. Yet, Adam also sinned against God by eating the same fruit. Why? The answer is love, and love makes people do things they normally would not do. For example, in Judges 14:12-18, Samson told a group of thirty Philistine men a riddle and said he would reward each of them with a robe and a set of clothing if they could tell him the answer to his riddle within seven days of his marriage feast, which he celebrated with them. Otherwise, each of them would have to give him a robe and a set of clothing. Out of love for his wife, who was also a Philistine, Samson eventually gave in and told her the answer to his riddle. Then, Samson's wife in turn told the Philistine men the answer. As a result, Samson lost the bet.

How do we know love was also at play in Adam's case? The Bible tells us that Adam just accepted the fruit from Eve and ate without hesitation or questioning (Genesis 3:6). No believer in their right mind (a mind governed by the Spirit of God) would do something that they were specifically instructed not to do. But because Adam was so emotionally in love with Eve, his mind was completely preoccupied with her instead of what God said about eating from the Tree of Knowledge and its consequences. Thus, he welcomed the fruit given to him by Eve and ate it without uttering a word.

The supposition above is highly probable because Eve was made for Adam and presented to him in Genesis 2:21-22, which was after God had already given Adam the command to not eat from the Tree of Knowledge in Genesis 2:17. According to Genesis 12:11, 14, and 19, Sarai, the 65-year-old wife of Abram, was so beautiful that Pharaoh of Egypt took her to be his wife. So although the Bible does not provide any details of Eve's physical beauty, it is not unreasonable to say that Eve must have been the most beautiful woman to have ever been created by God. Therefore, Eve would have been all that was on Adam's mind—not God's command. And because the only kind of love that mankind knows is the love that is associated with the flesh (love by way of one or more of the five physical senses: seeing, hearing, feeling, tasting, and smelling), Adam's downfall was also due to his mind being governed by his flesh. After all, Adam's initial connection to Eve was through "sight" when she was first brought to him by God.

Concerning our financial health, the very first step to attaining financial victory is budgeting (which I'll talk more about in Chapter VI). This is why in Luke 14:28-30 Jesus said, *"Suppose one of you wants to build a tower. Won't you first sit down and estimate the cost to see if you have enough money to complete it? For if you lay the foundation and are not able to finish it, everyone who sees it will ridicule you, saying, 'This person began to build and wasn't able to finish.'"* Budgeting is making sure we have money to not only cover our needs, debts, and wants but also save and invest for the future. However, many of us do not budget.

Why do we not budget? Because budgeting is not a desire of our flesh. Instead, the flesh yearns to spend without boundaries or constraints, which is associated with the characteristics of pride, foolishness, and ignorance—all of which lend to financial difficulty. As such, this desire eventually gives rise to a stronghold of unrestrained spending (spending more than what one makes or can afford), which is how many of us get into trouble with credit cards. Though we want to have money to cover our living expenses and still be able to save (which is our spirit's willingness to do what God desires), we can't as long as our mind is ruled by our flesh, which wants to spend without restrictions because of the sin in us.

Why Is the Mind So Drawn to the Flesh?

To understand why the mind is so naturally drawn to the flesh, I will use a chemistry concept known as electronegativity to help explain. In the field of chemistry, electronegativity refers to the tendency of an atom to attract or pull an electron towards it. The higher the electronegativity value of an atom, the stronger it is at attracting an electron towards itself. For example, sodium chloride (NaCl), which is also known as table salt, is made up of two atoms: sodium (Na) and chlorine

(Cl). Na's electronegativity is 0.9 and Cl's is 3.0 (on a scale of 0.7 to 4.0). Because of the higher electronegativity of Cl, an electron is naturally attracted to the Cl atom but not to Na. That's why in chemistry, we see the ions of NaCl denoted as Na⁺ and Cl⁻. The superscript minus symbol on Cl represents the electron that is pulled away from Na's outer shell and is now a part of Cl's valence.

Likewise, if we have to assign a numerical value to the strengths of the desires of the flesh and those of God (using the electronegativity scale), the former would be 4.0 and the latter 0.7. Therefore, like an electron, the mind is naturally drawn towards the desires of the flesh instead of God because these fleshly desires are stronger or higher in priority. Why are the desires of the flesh so strong? Satan's lies make the desires of the flesh very strong and attractive. Looking back at Eve, the lies the Devil told her did two things: They stirred up her fleshly desires for the fruit of the Tree of Knowledge, and they magnified those desires in her. The more Eve looked at the forbidden tree with respect to the lies she was told, the stronger her desire for its fruit became.

As a financial example, let's say Moab wants a big-screen TV—that's his fleshly desire. As he is looking at such a TV, a salesperson begins to tell him all these amazing features about the TV. The more he looks at the TV with respect to the sales pitch from the salesperson, the greater the desire he has for wanting to buy the TV. Before the salesperson started talking, Moab had a desire to own a big-screen TV. But it wasn't until the salesperson began telling Moab how wonderful the TV was that his desire for it became stronger and stronger.

How Is a Stronghold Formed?

Concerning the human soul, a stronghold is a habitual pattern of thoughts within a person's mind that leads them to repeat an action that is sinful or does not conform to God's nature in the absence of the Enemy's direct influence. It is important to understand that Satan is the one who initially plants such thoughts that give rise to a stronghold in the mind of a person by way of his lies. The purpose of the Enemy sowing these thoughts into our minds is to stir up and magnify ungodly desires within our flesh and to get us to act on those desires.

Although it can be difficult to pinpoint exactly which thought or thoughts were directly planted in a person's mind by the Devil or his fallen angels, it is safe to say that all human thoughts that are contrary to God have a satanic origin. In other words, whether the opposing thought or thoughts were brought on or planted by the Evil One himself, evil spirits, people, or other stimuli (e.g., the news, social media, movies, images, writings, etc.), all of these triggers point back to Satan. Why? Because it was the Serpent who initially introduced sin to mankind when he deceived Eve (Genesis 3:1-6), and the fact that Satan is the prince of the air (Ephesians 2:2) and the ruler of this world (1 John 5:19, 2 Corinthians 4:4).

So, how does a stronghold arise? First, contrary thoughts are planted in a person's mind by Satan via his lies. The lies stimulate thoughts in the mind of a person and convince them to act (by way of their will) according to a desire or desires of their flesh. The resulting pleasure, satisfaction, or comfort from the ungodly action, in turn, reinforces the opposing thoughts that were initially planted in their mind (after one occurrence or repeats of the behavior) leading to the establishment of a stronghold. The greater the perceived pleasure, satisfaction, or comfort from the activity, the stronger the stronghold becomes over time. As such, a stronghold enslaves the individual's mind to obey their flesh as well as the Enemy. Because of this, a person repeats the same evil or contrary behavior over and over again.

Therefore, a stronghold acts as a fortress to preserve the long-term effect of Satan's initial influences on a person's mind and his control over the individual's life. For this reason, it is not necessary for the Enemy to continually exert his evil control on the mind. Once a stronghold is raised, it automatically carries on the will of the Enemy in the person whose mind is ruled by their flesh without further direct influences from the Serpent.

Unlike God, the Devil is not omniscient (all-knowing); therefore, he cannot know what's in our minds or hearts—which are our thoughts. How do we know this? 1 Kings 8:39 says, *"Forgive and act; deal with everyone according to all they do since you [God] know their hearts (for you alone know every human heart)."* According to this verse, only God knows our thoughts. Nevertheless, Satan is aware of the fleshly desires in us because he is the father of all ungodly impulses. For example, some desires of the Enemy are violence, covetousness, disobedience, stealing, and destruction (Ezekiel 28:16-18, Isaiah 14:12-14, John 8:44, John 10:10). In addition, the Evil One has been roaming around the Earth for a very long time observing (Job 1:7, Job 2:2) and influencing the lives of many individuals (Genesis 3:1-6, Job 1, 1 Chronicles 21:1, Matthew 16:22-23, Luke 22:3-5, Acts 5:1-4). Thus, he is very good at predicting the behaviors or actions of human beings.

From a financial point of view, Satan knows that the flesh desires to gratify the self instead of making financial sacrifices. This yearning, which is due to pride, foolishness, and ignorance of the flesh, is in direct opposition to what God says in Proverbs 21:20: *"The wise store up choice food and olive oil, but fools gulp theirs down."* From a financial perspective, this scripture exhorts us to save and not to spend everything we make or exceed our financial means. Because the Enemy is well aware of our fleshly desire to please ourselves as just stated, he takes advantage of this desire to influence our mind to get us to act on the craving or stir up such desire to establish, for instance, a stronghold of impulsive buying (which is making unplanned purchases). The Serpent's goal is to eventually get us to not save and spend more than what we bring in.

For example, Omri goes out to the local grocery store to buy formulas and diapers for his newborn. While he is there, Omri passes by the snacks and drinks section; he picks up $30 worth of these things along with his baby items, which already cost $100. As he gets gasoline for his new $40,000 vehicle, Omri sees an advertisement for pizzas on the storefront and decides to pick up $50 worth of pizzas for his family on top of the $60 gasoline charge. As Omri makes his way home, a friend phones him about the latest action movie coming out, and Omri stops at his local theater to snatch up two tickets, each costing $15, for him and his wife for the 8 p.m. Friday night show. So Omri spent $110 more than what he needed to today. This has been a habit of Omri's for a few years now. Because of this, he's always buying things beyond what he needs. Hence, Omri has no savings and has already maxed out two credit cards totaling $7,000.

In the case of Omri, the lies of the Enemy came to him in the forms of images, things, and both written and spoken words. These lies led to the formation of thoughts in Omri's mind which stirred up and magnified his fleshly desires to buy things. As his spending behavior continued, it reinforced and solidified the habitual pattern of thoughts or stronghold of impulsive buying in Omri's mind. This impulsive buying then developed into a stronghold of unrestrained spending, which was how Omri ended up with a balance of $7,000 on two credit cards.

The Grip of Strongholds

One of the goals of the Serpent is to erect as many strongholds as he can over a person's mind. He knows that the more strongholds he can raise, the harder it will be for the individual to escape his control. So far, I have talked about the strongholds of unrestrained spending and impulsive buying. Another stronghold that keeps individuals in financial hardship or from improving their financial position is the stronghold of financial ignorance. As I previously stated, pride, foolishness, and ignorance are characteristics of the flesh that lead to financial difficulty. Of these traits, ignorance can greatly help the Devil to hurt a person financially. The word "ignorance" does not mean stupid. It means a lack of knowledge or not knowing the truth due to not yet having learned.

Again, Satan is aware that we are prideful, foolish, and ignorant because he is the father of these ungodly traits. Specifically concerning ignorance of the flesh, the Enemy will plant thoughts in a person's mind to distract or keep them from acquiring God's financial truths, so that they remain exactly where they are: financially ignorant. The more their mind is kept preoccupied with other things, the less they will be interested in learning about God's financial principles on how to be a good financial steward until it's too late. This is how the Enemy raises a stronghold of financial ignorance in the mind of the person.

The stronghold of financial ignorance is very destructive. Hosea 4:6 tells us, *"My people [believers] are destroyed for lack of knowledge."* Remember the servant in the Parable of the Talents who received one talent from his master and hid it in the ground instead of investing it? This servant's financial ignorance kept him from knowing how to manage the talent that was given to him and allowed the Devil to destroy him instead. The one talent this servant had was eventually taken away from him, and he was then thrown out of his master's house into the darkness. Although Hosea 4:6 is specifically pointing to believers, the message applies to all people. No one is exempt from destruction due to lack of knowledge.

When we reject God's financial truths—that is, we don't read and study the Bible and apply its money principles—we are essentially giving the Enemy permission and authority to rule over our financial life just like the servant that was given the one talent. Thus, Satan's grip over our mind through the many strongholds only tightens keeping us in bondage to financial difficulty or from improving our financial situation.

We Make the Choices to Rob and Destroy Ourselves

Although Satan is the culprit behind all spiritual assaults—that is, he is the one who puts forth into play the deceptions and lies against mankind—*we* ultimately make the choices to rob and destroy ourselves. Nowhere in the account of Adam and Eve's fall from paradise did the Devil force the duo to commit sin. Additionally, there was no pressure present to influence Eve to disobey God. Furthermore, Eve had complete control over her choice. Yet, she chose to eat from the forbidden tree. Then, Eve gave Adam some of the fruit and he, whose ability to choose was fully intact, also chose to eat (without any pressure). Because they have free will, Adam and Eve could have chosen to not eat from the Tree of Knowledge. But instead, they both willfully chose to sin against God.

What is said about Adam and Eve is also true of other biblical cases of spiritual influence and/or attack as well. In Job's situation, the Sabeans and Chaldeans killed many of Job's servants and made off with his animals (Job 1:15, 17), a wind came and caused his eldest son's house to collapse killing all his children (Job 1:18-19), and Job himself came down with sores (Job 2:7)—all of which were the works of the Devil (Job 1:12, Job 2:6). Although there was great pressure from the tragedies that befell Job, he still had total control over his free will and chose not to sin against God (Job 1:22, Job 2:10). At the end of his story, God restored everything that Job had lost.

In Acts 5:1-10, Ananias and his wife Sapphira decided to sell a piece of their land for money and gave the proceeds to the apostles' cause. However, the couple also decided to keep a portion of the profit and made it sound like the money given to the apostles was all of the proceeds from the sale of their property. Verse 3 made it very clear that Satan was the one who filled their minds (hearts) with the idea of lying to the apostles and the Holy Spirit. However, nothing in the entire account indicated that the Enemy forced Ananias and Sapphira to lie. Additionally, unlike in Job's case, there was no external pressure to influence their decisions to lie about the monetary giving. Yet, they willfully chose to sin against God (verse 2) despite having 100% control over their choices. Because of their sin, they died.

The same argument above invariably applies to the financial woes we, including myself, bring upon ourselves. Though Satan is the mastermind behind all financial deceptions, we ultimately make the choices or decisions that lead to robbing and destroying our financial health. In many of these financial choice and decision-making instances, much like that of Ananias and his wife, we also have full control over our finances and zero external pressure. Recall that I lost $8,000 in an IPO investment (as told in the introduction of this book), Ahaziah from Chapter II racked up $400,000 of debt, and Omri developed a stronghold of unrestrained spending resulting in a total charge of $7,000 on his credit cards. How did all of this happen? Though influenced by the Enemy, each of us freely made the choices or decisions that led to putting ourselves in the financial states we were in.

CHAPTER V

BREAKING THE SPIRITUAL CYCLE OF FINANCIAL DECEPTION

Victory Begins with Faith

Since Satan is the source of all our financial woes, to cast him and his spiritual influences out of our financial life, we must put on the full armor of God. As Christians, we have access to this spiritual armor the moment we accept Jesus Christ as our Lord and Savior. But why the armor of God? Because our Enemy is not flesh and blood but an evil spirit (Ephesians 6:12). Therefore, we cannot battle our foe with physical weapons. The only way to fight him is in the spirit and with the armor of God.

However, donning the armor of God is not as simple as putting on a shirt or a pair of shoes. Though our spirit is willing to put on the armor of God, our flesh rejects the armor. That is why Galatians 5:17 says, "...*The flesh desires what is contrary to the Spirit, and the Spirit what is contrary to the flesh.*" Because our flesh always seeks that which is counter to God, it will always reject the armor of God, and our spirit can do nothing about it. So although we have access to the armor, our flesh prevents our spirit from putting it on. Thus, we cannot use its spiritual powers to overcome the financial darkness in our lives. If taking up the armor of God was as easy as putting on a shirt, most Christians would have very few problems in their lives.

So, how can we then put on the armor of God so that we can break the Enemy's cycle of deception? Only our faith in God will enable us to put on the armor. We must understand that donning the armor of God signifies that we are willing to and will do what God desires, which our flesh does not want to do. In Chapter IV, I mentioned two very important financial truths—budgeting (Luke 14:28) and financial sacrifice (Proverbs 21:20)—that are necessary or even required to change one's financial situation for the better. But I also said that many of us don't budget and make financial sacrifices because these things are not desires of the flesh but of God. Therefore, many of us would rather spend without constraint and satisfy ourselves now than budget and make sacrifices.

Hebrews 11:1 tells us, "*...Faith is confidence in what we hope for and assurance about what we do not see.*" In other words, faith is "more than" just believing. Even Satan and his demonic underlings believed there is a God. In the simplest terms, faith is:

- Unquestioning belief in the existence of God
- Trusting in the Word of God that what it says is true (this is analogous to putting one's entire weight on a chair without thinking when one sits on it)

- Being able to see ourselves at the finish line as He sees us—in this case, financially victorious
- Be willing to do what God commands
- Being obedient in carrying out those commands even though the promise of God's truths—victory in our finances—have yet to materialize

How does believing, trusting, and seeing that we already have financial victory even before we have it make any sense? The Bible tells us that God does not and cannot lie. Numbers 23:19 echoes this truth: *"God is not human, that he should lie, not a human being, that he should change his mind. Does he speak and then not act? Does he promise and not fulfill?"* If we are willing and obedient, what He promises will come, whether today or five years from now, because it already belongs to us.

For example, in Joshua 6:2-20, God told Joshua and his men (including seven priests with trumpets of rams' horns) to march around the city of Jericho once for six days. During each of these days, only the sounds of the trumpets were to be heard. Then, on the seventh day, they were to march around Jericho seven times also with the trumpets blowing. When the priests blew a long blast on the seventh march around, Joshua was instructed to have his troops shout very loud. At that moment, the wall of Jericho will collapse and the city will be theirs for the taking as God had promised. The Israelite men did exactly as they were commanded by God even though they had not yet seen the wall of Jericho fall and claimed victory as God had promised them. Why? They fully trusted the Lord and could see it in their minds or from God's perspective that the city's wall had already fallen and victory was already theirs. Thus, they were willing and obedient. This is what it means to "...*walk by faith, not by [physical] sight*" (2 Corinthians 5:7). Of course, what God promised to Joshua and the Israelites here did come to pass.

Every Christian has a measure of faith (Romans 12:3). However, not every believer will trust in God, see things His way, and/or be willing and obedient. Sometimes, a follower is obedient in doing what God wants, but they have no trust in the Lord and do not see things from His point of view or are not willing to. Hence, only faith that leads to having a relationship with the Lord drives us—our mind—to trust in Him, see things His way, and be willing and obedient. This is the kind of faith that has the power to negate our flesh's opposition to the armor of God and enable our spirit to take up the spiritual armor. When we have a relationship with the Lord, His desires are stronger or higher in priority to us than the desires of our flesh. Hence, our mind will become naturally attracted to God and His desires through our spirit.

So not only did Joshua and the Israelite men from the example above believed and trusted in God and saw their situation from God's eyes, but His desire for them to have Jericho was also very strong in Joshua and his men.

Growing and Developing Our Faith

As followers of the One True God, what can we do to grow and develop our faith (which is a spiritual force) so that it becomes the kind of faith that leads to trusting in the Lord, seeing ourselves as He sees us, and becoming willing and obedient? We must feed our spirit with "spiritual food"—that is, we must be in the Word, have an active prayer life, and fellowship. These are the things that will enable us to develop a deeper connection or relationship with the Lord God through our faith and draw our mind closer to Him, which will then enable us to break the Enemy's cycle of financial deception.

As Christians, the purpose of being in the Word is to renew our minds. Romans 12:2 says, *"Do not conform to the pattern of this world, but be transformed by the renewing of your mind."* In other words, we must do away with our old thinking and thoughts, fill our minds with truths, and see things God's way. Only when our mind is rewired in this way can our faith start to grow. If there is no renewal of the mind, there will be no change of the heart. So, what does this mean? It means, *"Though seeing, [we] do not see; though hearing, [we] do not hear or understand..."* (Matthew 13:13) because our spiritual eyes and ears are still closed. Thus, there is no growth in the faith. As such, there will be no increase in trust in the Lord and an unwillingness to act since we do not see things His way. The Enemy hopes that we do not grow and develop in the faith so that we do not improve our financial situations.

The Bible is the ultimate blueprint for righteous and successful living in every area of life, including our finances. When we begin to apply God's truths, that's when we will start to see how the Lord is moving in us. As we witness the positive changes in our life, our faith in God strengthens. By immersing ourselves in the Bible regularly, we are developing a relationship with the Lord. Unless we are rooted in God like the branches are to a vine, we will not see things from a spiritual perspective and be willing and be compelled to act.

As such, we will not bear fruit in our life. Jesus reinforced this sentiment in John 15:5-6 when he said, *"I am the vine; you [believers] are the branches. If you remain in me and I in you, you will bear much fruit; apart from me you can do nothing."*

Prayer is more than just a way for us to communicate with God. When we pray, we invite the Lord Almighty into our spiritual life. As we begin to pray regularly, our relationship with God will strengthen and our faith will also start to grow. As Christians, we should *"pray continually"* (1 Thessalonians 5:17) in everything that we do. We ought to follow the example of the Prophet Daniel, who got on his knees three times a day and prayed to the Lord (Daniel 6:10) even while he was an exile of Judah and chief administrator of the whole Medo-Persian empire. In his position of chief administrator, Daniel could have been arrogant; but he chose not to be. Instead, Daniel continued to give praise and thanks to God in his daily prayers as well as ask Him for guidance. In doing so, his faith in the Lord only grew and became stronger.

How do we know that prayer develops our faith? Daniel was well-liked and favored by the king of the empire he was serving. Because of this, the other administrators were jealous of him and sought to get Daniel killed. So they deceived the king into issuing an edict that dictated that all must only pray to him for thirty days. When Daniel was found violating this decree, he was put into the lions' den. However, because of his unwavering faith in God, Daniel expressed no anger towards the king as well as the officials who put him in his predicament. At the same time, Daniel also showed no fear of the fact that he was in the presence of hungry lions. We know this to be true because of how Daniel answered the king (the morning after he was placed in the den) in Daniel 6:21-22 when he said, *"May the king live forever! My God sent his angel, and he shut the mouths of the lions. They have not hurt me, because I was found innocent in his sight."* This passage tells us that Daniel was completely calm and that his faith was very strong in God, which was only possible because of the relationship Daniel had with the Lord through his daily prayer life.

As an individual Christian, it is very important that you fellowship with other believers. In Genesis 2:18, God said it was not good for Adam to be alone. That was why He created Eve to be Adam's companion so that the two could learn from each other and lean on one another. It would be most beneficial for you, especially if you are a new believer or struggling in the faith, to fellowship with other believers who are strong in the faith. In other words, you should fellowship with other believers who immerse themselves in the Word and practice what the Bible says. Why is this important? Because someone who is blind—that is, they do not know and practice the truths—cannot lead another who is also blind; for if they do, both will fall into a pit (Luke 6:39). Therefore, fellowshipping with others who are actively in the Word and practicing the truths is critical.

When we fellowship, we are helping to spiritually build up one another as 1 Thessalonians 5:11 exhorts us to do. The ones who are stronger in the faith can help to pull up those who are new or struggling in the faith. Elisha's close fellowship with Elijah, for example, greatly helped him to become stronger in the faith, which enabled Elisha to carry on the mantle of Elijah after he was taken up to Heaven by God. Therefore, by fellowshipping, we learn from one another as well as help each other to grow and develop in the faith. When Christians come together like this, the Enemy trembles in fear.

Humility Over Pride

In the introduction and previous chapters, I mentioned that pride was a trait that led to financial difficulty. When we think of the word pride, things like "having a high opinion of oneself, being proud of one's accomplishments, or conceitedness" come to mind. But pride is more than these things; pride is about putting our desires above God's desires. How is this so? Because that's exactly what Adam and Eve, the first humans, did. The pair were told not to eat from the Tree of Knowledge by God, but they ate from it anyway because they put their desires above God's—that's pride.

Concerning our financial health/success, these are the things God desires for us:

- That we put God first (Matthew 6:33)
- That we seek financial knowledge and wisdom (Proverbs 4:6-7)
- That we set financial parameters through budgeting (Luke 14:28)
- That we make sacrifices now and save (Proverbs 21:20)
- That we not be slaves to debt (Proverbs 22:7)
- That we build wealth gradually by investing wisely (Proverbs 13:11 ESV, Ecclesiastes 11:2)

- That *"...we are more than conquerors through him [Christ] who loved us"* (Romans 8:37)

However, the pride of the flesh (which is 100% contrary to the Spirit [Galatians 5:17]):

- Loves money
- Rejects financial knowledge and wisdom
- Desires to spend without boundaries
- Wants to satisfy the self now (greed)
- Wants to borrow without restriction
- Seeks to make a lot of money fast (though it's unrealistic—I'll explain this in Chapter VIII)
- Desires to quit when things get tough

When our mind is governed by the pride of our flesh, we place the desires of our flesh above God's desires. This is why many born-again believers have financial problems. Pride is the number one enemy that keeps us from living the financial life God intends for us. In fact, pride is the single factor that enables Satan to defeat a believer every single time.

To put the pride of the flesh in check, we must understand and have humility, which can only be imparted to us by the Holy Spirit. By definition, humility means to be humbled or not think highly of oneself. However, humility goes beyond that; it is about putting God's desires above ours. For example, Joseph, the son of Jacob and Rachel, who was sold into slavery by his very own brothers because of their jealousy and hatred of him, was very humble despite everything that had happened to him. Because of Joseph's humbleness to himself and the Lord, God blessed Joseph while he was an Egyptian slave. As such, he was well-liked by those around him. Ultimately, God enabled Joseph to become Prime Minister of Egypt after he interpreted the meaning behind Pharaoh's dreams, which was that a famine would soon be coming, and advised the Egyptian ruler of what must be done for his country to be saved.

Because he was very humble, Joseph put God's desires over his. Some of the things that God desires of his children are for us to honor our father and mother (Exodus 20:12), to not commit adultery and steal (Exodus 20:14-15), and to not do evil to others who have done evil to us (Romans 12:17). The Bible shows us that Joseph had great love and respect for his father Jacob regardless of what happened to him in life. When Jacob finally came to Egypt, Joseph threw his arms around his father and cried for a long time. In addition, Joseph agreed to lay Jacob to rest where his fathers, Isaac and Abraham, were buried (which was a cave in the field of Machpelah) when the day came. Moreover, when Jacob finally died, Joseph threw himself on his father, wept, kissed him, and mourned him for over three months before burying his father as he had promised.

Before Joseph was promoted to the second highest Egyptian office by Pharaoh, he was a slave of Potiphar, the captain of Pharaoh's guard, who bought him from the Ishmaelites. While in Potiphar's house, Joseph was put in charge of everything and he took very good care of all that belonged to his master. Potiphar saw that Joseph was very trustworthy, and he did not concern himself with the things of his house. When his master's wife tried daily to get Joseph to go to bed with her, instead of committing adultery and sinning against God, he always refused. Although Joseph's flesh desired to steal from

Potiphar and sleep with his master's wife, he chose to do what was right because he placed God's desires above his.

For what his brothers did to him, Joseph, as the second most powerful person in Egypt, could have easily thrown them into prison for life or executed them right on the spot when they came to his country to buy grain. But Joseph had great humility; he never used his position to pay back his brothers for doing him wrong after he reunited with them and even after his father died. Joseph instead showered them with great love and kindness, which fulfills the commandments to love God and to love people (Matthew 22:36-39).

The kind of humility Joseph exhibited could only come from having a deeply rooted relationship with the Lord of all creation. If we desire to be free of the Enemy's cycle of financial deception or to be truly financially prosperous, we must have humility. To have such humility, we must yield our mind to the Holy Spirit, who is our helper and can bestow to us such a gift.

Be Willing and Obedient

As I said, putting on the armor of God signifies that we are willing to and will do what God wants instead of what we want. Or, as James 1:22 puts it: *"Do not merely listen to the word, and so deceive yourselves. Do what it says."* The Bible talks about the different pieces of the armor of God in Ephesians 6:14-17. When the Apostle Paul penned this section of the Scripture on the armor of God, he was imagining the armor with respect to a Roman soldier's outfit and combat gear.

From the aforementioned passage, it tells us that six pieces of equipment comprise the armor of God.

The first piece of the armor is the belt of truth (Ephesians 6:14). Concerning the subject matter of this book, the belt represents knowledge of God's financial truths. Of all the pieces of the armor of God, the belt of truth is by far the most important and the piece by which all the others hang on. Why? For all the other pieces to work, the belt of truth must first be properly secure to our spiritual waist. What does this mean though? It means that we must first acquire the knowledge of the truths concerning the management of money. Knowledge of the truths is what fuels the armor of God. The financial field is vast and constantly expanding. So the belt of truth calls for us to continuously learn and seek out God's financial truths to stay abreast. Why is doing this important? Ecclesiastes 7:12 tells us, *"Wisdom is a shelter as money is a shelter, but the advantage of knowledge is this: Wisdom preserves those who have it."* In other words, financial knowledge and wisdom protect our lives and keep us from losing or wasting the money God entrusted to us.

The next piece is the breastplate of righteousness (Ephesians 6:14), which symbolizes living right according to the Word of God. From a financial point of view, it is the handling of our financial affairs according to the financial truths in the Bible. Luke 14:28 states, *"Suppose one of you wants to build a tower. Won't you first sit down and estimate the cost to see if you have enough money to complete it?"* and Proverbs 21:20 tells us, *"The wise store up choice food and olive oil, but fools gulp theirs down."* By putting on the breastplate of righteousness over our spiritual upper torso, we are signifying that we will create a budget to make sure we have money to not only cover our needs, debts, and wants but also to save and invest for our future. If we do not have enough money to cover our living expenses and save and invest, we then will make financial sacrifices to meet these financial requirements. Thus, wearing the breastplate of righteousness indicates that we are willing and will act on God's financial truths instead of what our flesh desires.

The helmet of salvation (Ephesians 6:17) is the third piece of the armor of God and is worn over our spiritual head. The helmet of salvation protects our mind and guards it against the lies from the Enemy that would create confusion and uncertainty about money and financial prosperity. As I discussed in Chapter III, Satan will do everything he can to sow confusion into our mind to keep us in financial darkness because he hates seeing us live financially prosperous. When we have on the helmet of salvation, it signifies that we will fill our mind with Bible truths relating to finance and meditate on them so that should the Evil One attack our financial positions, our mind will have no room for his lies. With our mind filled with the truths, *"We demolish arguments and every pretension that sets itself up against the knowledge of God, and we take captive every thought to make it obedient to Christ"* (2 Corinthians 10:5).

Remember, the Devil's lies only have power if they can enter and convince our mind to dictate to our will to oppose God. Therefore, like a physical shield, the shield of faith (Ephesians 6:16) helps to defend us against the lies of the

Enemy by halting or deflecting them. In this way, the shield of faith prevents the lies of the Evil One from ever reaching our mind. The larger and thicker the shield of faith is, the more effective it is at defending against Satan's lies. One way for a believer to level up their shield of faith is for them to fellowship with other Christians who are mature in the faith and living according to Bible truths and godly financial principles. In this way, the individuals who are stronger in the faith are helping to build up the shield of faith of the one who is weaker.

The fifth piece of the armor of God is the shoes of the gospel of peace (Ephesians 6:15). The shoes are like the rock on which a wise man built his house so that when rain and winds come against it, the house does not fall (Matthew 7:24-25). Hence, when these shoes are fitted to our spiritual feet, they indicate that we are well grounded in God's financial truths; therefore, we will not be swayed by Satan's lies. Additionally, with these shoes on, we are always ready to dispel the lies of the Enemy and "*...go into all the world and preach the gospel [including its financial truths] to all creation*" (Mark 16:15).

Finally, the sword of the Spirit (Ephesians 6:17), which is the sixth piece of the armor of God, is the most powerful armament of the armor because it represents the Word of God or God's truths on the subject matter of finance in action. The sword of the Spirit is so powerful that whenever it is drawn from its pouch, it emits a mighty ray of light that exposes the deceptions and lies of the Devil immediately giving them no chance to influence us. Hebrews 4:12 tells us, "*...The word of God is alive and active. Sharper than any double-edged* *sword, it penetrates even to dividing soul and spirit, joints and marrow.*" So, what does this mean? It means that the moment our spirit swings the sword (which is truth) against the Enemy, it instantly frees us from his deceptions, lies, and strongholds. No longer will we be confused and/or be in bondage to financial darkness. However, for the sword to be powerful in the manner described, we must know God's financial truths and practice them routinely in our financial life.

Isaiah 1:19 says, "*If you are willing and obedient, you will eat the good things of the land.*" To eat the good things of the land—that is, to get victory in your finances—you must put on the full armor of God.

Stay in God's Plan No Matter What

God wants the very best for us more so than we ever want for ourselves. That's why in Jeremiah 29:11 God said, "*...I know the plans [for all areas of life] I have for you... plans to prosper you and not to harm you, plans to give you hope and a future.*" Indeed, the Lord does have a plan—it's His Word and His financial truths as discussed in this book—to ensure that we have financial victory over the Evil One. Those who are faithful and abide by God's plan are never disappointed in the outcome, but those who decide to deviate from His plan often find themselves in misery or unsuccessful.

There were individuals in the Bible who were faithful and stayed in God's plan as well as those that did not. Two examples representing each side of the extreme were Abraham and King Saul. God had plans for each of them: For Abraham, God wanted to make him into a great nation, make his name great, and bless all people on Earth through him (Genesis 12:2). As for Saul, the Lord desired to make him into a great king and have his kingship endured forever (1 Samuel 13:3). To put His plan into motion for Abraham, God commanded Abraham to leave his home country and go to the land in which God would give to him and his descendants. Although Abraham knew not where he was going, he obeyed God and left on the journey.

Throughout his migration, Abraham was completely obedient to the Lord in doing everything He instructed. How do we know this? In Genesis 26:5 God said, "*...Abraham obeyed me and did everything I required of him, keeping my commands, my decrees, and my instructions.*" This statement was made to Isaac, the son of Abraham, well after Abraham had already died. Of course, Abraham was extremely blessed by God during his lifetime. He accumulated great wealth and had children in his old age.

Although Abraham never saw the great nation his offspring became, his name became great, and all people on Earth be blessed through him (all of which did come to pass through his descendants King David and the Lord Jesus Christ), he was still willing and obedient and stayed in God's plan. Why? Because Abraham set his mind on the eternal plan of God instead of his fleshly desires. Thus, the Enemy could not deceive Abraham into getting out of God's plan. Romans 8:5 tells us, "*...Those who live according to the Spirit have their minds set on what the Spirit desires*"—and Abraham was one of these individuals. Because of his unwavering faith in the Lord, Abraham is known as the father of the Christian faith.

King Saul, on the other hand, decided that he was going to handle things his way. Saul had a great start in his walk with the Lord in that there was no one among God's people at the time whom He desired more to become king of Israel than Saul. However, Saul began to spiral downhill when he decided to do the work of priest by performing a burnt offering to receive favor from God to help him defeat his enemy, the Philistines, when Samuel did not come to Saul at the set time. This act of Saul violated the Mosaic laws which explicitly stated that only those of the Levite lineage can be priests and do such work (Numbers 1:48-53, 8:19; Deuteronomy 10:8). In addition, by taking the matter into his own hands, Saul directly disobeyed Samuel's command (which came from God) as instructed in 1 Samuel 10:8. Thus, Saul's action angered God.

As a second chance to redeem himself, the Lord ordered Saul to go and annihilate the Amalekites, the people who ambushed the weary Israelites when they were coming out of Egyptian slavery led by Moses more than 400 years earlier. Saul did attack the Amalekites as he was told by God, but he did not wipe them out completely as commanded. Saul brought back their king, Agag, and the best of their animals. Because of his disobedience, Saul got out of God's plan to make him into a great king. Thus, God abandoned him.

Why did Saul go against God's commands? Because his mind believed the lies of Satan, and his mind was ruled by his flesh. The Enemy's lies were presented to Saul in the size of the Philistines' army ("...*three thousand chariots, six thousand charioteers, and soldiers as numerous as the sand on the seashore*" [1 Samuel 13:5]), the sight of his troops in fear and scattering (1 Samuel 13:8, 11), and the belief that Saul was great himself without God (*"...he [Saul] set up a monument in his own honor..."* [1 Samuel 15:12]). Since he believed the lies, Saul feared that the Philistine troops might overrun his army; he bowed down to the pressures from those around him and his environment; and he became prideful (that's why he brought back Agag and the best of the Amalekites' animals as trophies of his victory). Fear, inability to deal with pressure/stress, and pride are all characteristics of the flesh, which Saul's mind was controlled by.

Romans 8:5 says, *"Those who live according to the flesh have their minds set on what the flesh desires."* Unlike Abraham, Saul's mind was focused on the things below instead of above. Because of this, he was easily deceived by Satan. In the end, Saul died by suicide and his kingship did not continue. This is why it's so important for us to grow our faith in God, develop a character of humility, and be willing and obedient to the Word. It's the only way to keep our mind on what's above. In doing so, we will remain steadfast in God's eternal plan for us.

As we can see, God keeps His promise to those who stay in His plan. Nevertheless, we have to understand that we live in a fallen world. There will be difficult times and challenges will arise. Because Satan is the master of this world, it is his purpose to make life as difficult as he can for us. That is why the making of a great nation or king takes time. Likewise, achieving victory in our financial health will also take time. But Proverbs 3:5-6 tells us, *"Trust in the Lord with all your heart and lean not on your own understanding; in all your ways submit to him, and he will make your paths straight."* No matter what happens along the way, we are to rely on God for our victory and not ourselves. God has the plan and His plan never fails!

Nevertheless, the Enemy will try to get us out of the Lord's plan. He will attack us from every angle to cause us to abandon our position in God, but 1 John 4:4 reminds us that we *"...are from God and... the one who is in [us—the Holy Spirit—] is greater than the one [Satan] who is in this world."* In addition, this is what Jesus said, *"I have given you authority to trample on snakes and scorpions and to overcome all the power of the enemy [Satan]; nothing will harm you"* (Luke 10:19). Thus, the only thing that can stop us from breaking the Enemy's cycle of financial deception and winning the spiritual battle for our financial health is ourselves—our own free will.

CHAPTER VI
PREPARING FOR FINANCIAL VICTORY

All Money and Wealth Belong to God

Before proceeding, we must understand that all the money and wealth on Earth belongs to God; none of it is ours. How do we know this? According to John 1:3, *"Through him [Jesus] all things [including money and wealth] were made; without Him, nothing was made that has been made"* and Psalm 24:1-2 tells us, *"The earth is the Lord's, and everything in it, the world, and all who live in it; for he founded it on the seas and established it on the waters."* So, what does this mean for us? This means that we are just stewards of His money. A steward is a person who manages property that belongs to someone else.

Let's say you have $100,000 and you put it in the bank. Is the $100,000 still yours or does the money now belong to the bank? The money is still yours, and the bank is only a steward of it while it's in the bank's possession. Not only that, but you expect the bank to manage your money well and not lose it.

The same is true with the money that is in your possession: The money still belongs to God, and you are just a steward of it. This is why God has a vested interest in our financial health—because it's His money that we have! Therefore, God expects us, His followers, to handle His money well while we are on this planet.

Creating a Budget Is Crucial

The first step to claiming victory in the spiritual battle for our financial health is to create a budget. Creating a budget is vital. In Luke 14:28-30 Jesus said, *"Suppose one of you wants to build a tower. Won't you first sit down and estimate the cost to see if you have enough money to complete it? For if you lay the foundation and are not able to finish it, everyone who sees it will ridicule you, saying, 'This person began to build and wasn't able to finish.'"* If God didn't think we needed to budget, Jesus would never have mentioned it. The purpose of a budget is threefold:

1. It allows us to see how much money is coming in, where all the income is going, and how much is left for savings.
2. The constraint of a budget helps us to develop financial discipline.
3. A budget enables us to identify where our financial problems lie so that we can begin to take steps to remedy them.

Satan does not want us to win the spiritual battle for our financial health. He knows that once Christians began to formulate a budget his defeat in this arena of spiritual warfare is nigh. The Serpent knows that by laying out our finances in front of us through a budget, we will know which area of our finances the Enemy has been deceiving us in. Thus, Satan will throw every lie he can at us to prevent or delay us from putting a budget together.

So, what goes into a budget? There are numerous ways to put a budget together. However, I suggest the creation of a budget be as simple as possible. Having said this, a budget should include the following financial parameters: income, needs, debts, wants, and savings. Together, the needs, debts, and wants comprise the cost of living. Our needs are things like rent, groceries, utilities, health insurance, and auto insurance; these are things we need to live or are required by law to have. Debts are money owed for a mortgage, auto loans, student loans, and credit cards. And wants, which are things we don't need to live or not required by law, refer to items such as eat-outs, entertainment, hobbies, and cable/internet.

For each of the financial parameters, I suggest using a monthly dollar figure. Why? Because most of us deal with our income and cost of living on a monthly basis. For example, for the needs and wants, tabulate how much is spent in each area per month according to the items that fall under that category. In other words, how much is the individual monthly cost of rent, utilities, groceries, health insurance, and car insurance? How much is appropriated for entertainment, eat-outs, hobbies, and cable/internet per month? For the debts category, list the minimum required payments for each debt that is owed, except for credit cards. For credit cards, the payment should be more than the minimum.

Then, provide a monthly total for the needs, debts, and wants and add all three of these amounts together to get the monthly cost of living. For the income figure, use monthly net income because this is the amount we take home after certain deductions (e.g., taxes, Social Security, and Medicare). Finally, subtract the monthly cost of living from the net income to see what is left that can go towards savings.

The monthly net income is usually fixed from month to month. However, the cost of living is not fixed due to variable and unexpected expenses like groceries, utilities, vacations, and car repairs. Thus, I suggest that it is best to track at least six months' worth of spending to determine the highest monthly cost of living. Do not include unexpected expenses like vacations or car repairs in the budget, as they are not recurring expenses. Once the highest monthly cost of living is determined, create a budget to ensure there is always enough money to cover the items of the budget.

For example, Jonadab, who is single, tracked his cost of living for six months. His monthly cost of living figures for the observed period were $3,100; $3,300; $3,050; $3,400; $3,100; and $3,250. Jonadab's net monthly income is usually $3,000. Since $3,400 was his highest monthly cost of living, Jonadab created a budget to reflect this living cost as shown:

Jonadab's Monthly Budget[a]		
Monthly Net Income $3,000		
Needs	**Debts[b]**	**Wants**
Rent: $650	Student loan: $500	Eat-outs: $200
Grocery: $550	Auto loan: $300	Entertainment: $400
Utility: $180	Credit card: $100	Hobbies: $100
Health Insurance: $120[c]		Cable/Internet: $100
Auto Insurance: $200		
Total = $1,700	Total = $900	Total = $800
Monthly Cost of Living $3,400		Savings -$400

a: Monthly budget based on the highest cost of living during a 6-month observation period
b: Minimum monthly required payments (excluding credit card, which more should be put towards)
c: Amount is before tax

Mathematically, financial hardship, living paycheck to paycheck, and financial victory are defined as follows:
- Financial hardship: monthly net income < monthly cost of living
- Living paycheck to paycheck: monthly net income = monthly cost living

- Financial victory: monthly net income > monthly cost of living

And, mathematically, the only way an individual can experience financial hardship or live paycheck to paycheck is either by spending more than or all of what they make or having an income that is low relative to the cost of living.

Now that we know what financial victory is, it is important to have a monthly net income goal. Without such a goal, there is no driving force to improve one's financial health. As a starting point, I suggest the income be set at least 10% higher than the highest monthly cost of living. Once a budget is created, take actions to change the income and/or the parameters that make up the cost of living until financial victory is achieved. It's very clear that Jonadab is experiencing financial hardship because his monthly cost of living each month during the six-month observation period exceeds his income.

I know that when it comes to budgeting, many financial experts like to promote rules like 50/40/10, 60/25/15, or 70/20/10 for where specific percentages of our income should be allocated with respect to our needs, debts, wants, and savings. However, I like to think of these rules as a "curse" like the Old Testament laws. Can we honestly say that our needs will always be 50%, our debts and wants 40%, and our savings 10%? No. Will trying to allocate money this way be easy to always do? Most likely not.

That is why the Israelites of Old Testament times could never fulfill the laws given to them—because no one could obey the laws perfectly. The same is true with us; there's no way we could fulfill every one of those laws either. That's why

Jesus came and simplified all the laws of the Old Testament into two commands for all of us under the New Testament: Love God and love people (Matthew 22:37-39). So when we align ourselves with or stay in God's plan for financial victory, we don't need to try and conform to these "religious" budgeting rules. We just need to remember one thing: Get our income to be at least 10% higher than our highest cost of living and maintain that gap.

But you must understand that attaining financial victory is not something that happens overnight. It will take time and challenges will arise. That is why it's so important to strengthen our faith in God and yield to the Holy Spirit. Abraham, Daniel, Joseph, and so many others who were victorious didn't get to where they were without challenges and obstacles. Just like us, they, too, lived in a broken world. For these individuals to endure and make it to the finish line, they have to have faith, be willing, and be obedient.

Financial Discipline is Paramount

This is what Hebrews 12:11 says about discipline: *"No discipline seems pleasant at the time, but painful. Later on, however, it produces a harvest of righteousness and peace for those who have been trained by it."* One of the main reasons why many Christians spend more than they make or can't save is because the flesh rejects this one truth of the Bible. Our flesh desires to spend without restriction, and the Enemy's objective is to get our mind to serve this desire of our flesh. Thus, when we spend more than we make, we begin to have financial problems. As I said, mathematically, it is impossible to have financial difficulty unless our cost of living is equal to or greater than our income.

Creating and having a budget in our financial life is one way for us to develop financial discipline in the area of spending, as it places constraints on how much money we spend on our needs, debts, and wants. Do not think for a second that a budget is only for the average believer or person. That is not true. Those who are wealthy remain so because they employ a budget to help them manage their money. There is no shame in using a budget. I can guarantee that folks like Abraham, Isaac, and Jacob all used a budget to help them control their money and wealth. How do we know this? Because that's how they remained wealthy until they parted from this Earth; and that's how they were able to transfer their wealth to their children's children just as a good man ought to do (Proverbs 13:22).

Of course, financial discipline is more than just controlling our spending. It also involves paying attention to where or how we spend our money. In other words, are we putting most of our money into assets or liabilities? Victory in our financial health is only possible if our money flows into more assets than liabilities. Assets generate income or increase in value, but liabilities do not.

Not only that, but we can't manage money well unless we know how. This is where financial knowledge and wisdom are critical in developing strong financial discipline. The Bible tells us, *"Do not forsake wisdom, and she will protect you; love her, and she will watch over you"* (Proverbs 4:6) and *"By wisdom, a house is built, and through understanding it is established; through knowledge its rooms are filled with rare and beautiful treasures"* (Proverbs 24:3-4). Every person who has victory in their finances possesses the right knowledge and wisdom to enable them to be in the financial position they are in. Therefore, *"Get [financial] wisdom. Though it cost all you have, get [financial] understanding"* (Proverbs 4:7).

Identifying the Spiritual Problems in Our Finance

If you are experiencing financial hardship or are currently living paycheck to paycheck, it's because Satan has been deceiving you in one or more of the following areas of your finances: income, needs, debts, wants, and/or savings.

At one point or another, many of us have thought to ourselves that we aren't good enough or can't do this or do that. This is exactly the kind of thinking Satan wants us to have to keep us from seeking a better-paying job, getting a promotion, or getting a new set of skills that can get us that higher-paying job. Thus, our income stays where it is and does not keep up with inflation or the increased cost of living. As such, we struggle to buy basic necessities (such as food and clothing) and can't save. So not only do we believe in and act on the lies of the Enemy that sound good (like I talked about in Chapter IV), but we also believe in and act on his lies that hold us back from improving or doing better. Remember Gideon? Satan lied to him that his clan was the weakest and that he was the least in his family. Had Gideon believed and acted on the lies, he would have been exactly what the Evil One wanted him to be.

Next up is our needs. Satan can easily trick us into thinking that we need something when we don't. For example, Jezebel decides to spend $500 on a purse because she believes it will make her stand out in front of all her friends despite working part-time making $20,000 a year and living with her parents. It was the Evil One who planted the thoughts in her mind that she needed this purse, but it was her flesh that wanted to look good. As with all things, the excitement is only temporary and will eventually fade. Thus, her expensive purse will only help her to be in the spotlight for about a week. After that, to keep her friends wowing again, Jezebel is going to need to buy another new $500 purse. This is the reason why miracles are not the main focus of Jesus's earthly ministry. He knows that the euphoria people get from seeing miracles does not last. Just look at Thomas, one of Christ's twelve disciples. He saw all of Jesus's amazing miracles, yet he still doubted.

When we really look at it, we see that there are only two kinds of debt. The first kind brings us income and/or builds equity for us (i.e., money borrowed for the purchases of a rental property and/or a home); and the second kind takes money out of our pocket and/or decreases in value over time (i.e., money borrowed to buy automobiles, sofas, and/or TVs). The Devil has been feeding our minds with lies to get us into the second type of debt. This explains why so many believers are struggling or drowning in debt.

For our wants, the Enemy has gotten us to believe that they are "needs" so we treat items in this area as "needs" when we really don't need them to live or they are not required by law. For example, we don't need to eat out every day or every week; buying groceries and cooking at home would be more beneficial to both our physical and financial health. But the

Evil One creates the illusion in our mind that we don't have time to cook, we can't cook, and/or it's just faster and cheaper to eat out. Thus, we keep pouring money into our wants, which is exactly what our flesh wants to do. Even money that's supposed to be for the rent, mortgage, grocery, utility, and/or car insurance goes into our wants too. It's no wonder many believers have financial difficulties. They have been deceived into believing that their wants are their needs.

Concerning savings, the Enemy has been telling us that we don't have to start saving (or save today) because there's always "next time." When the next pay period comes around, he tells us the same lie. Because we buy into the same lie over and over again, we do not save and continue to push it off.

The bottom line is that the Serpent has been deceiving us from the very beginning and our flesh is his ally. That's why many Christians continue to fall into the Devil's trap and experience never-ending financial darkness. No believer ever started off their life on Earth in financial distress; they got there because they were beguiled by the Evil One. Unfortunately for Satan though, God has provided us with a way to see right through his deceptions and lies with His financial truths. Through the work of Jesus, He exposed the Enemy for who he was and completely disarmed him. Through the Holy Spirit who now dwells in us, God has given us the power to win back our financial health and take back our financial life. We don't have to live in the dark anymore. We can choose to live in the light, starting today!

The Importance of Saving

We have to remember that we live in a fallen world and bad things can and will happen. We can lose our jobs at any time, we could get injured and not be able to work, or the company we work for could slash 50% of its workforce or go out of business. Not only that, but we may want to eventually retire and spend time with our family or go into ministry full-time serving the Lord. The loss of a job can be sudden and unexpected. We only need to look at what COVID-19 did to our economy in 2020. Millions of people lost their jobs overnight or in just a matter of a few weeks because the viral pandemic unexpectedly forced the closure of thousands of businesses.

When the things above happen, we are forced to fall back on our savings to meet our cost of living. All this is a fact of life in a world that is under the power of the Evil One. Therefore, we must make savings a priority. Always keep in mind that the Enemy wants us to do nothing until it's too late. So, how much should we be saving? Since the goal is to get our net monthly income to be at least 10% higher than our cost of living, this percentage will also serve as our monthly savings rate. For example, Deborah's monthly net income is $4,000 and her highest cost of living is $3,600. Therefore, she should allocate $400 into her savings every month.

God desires that we save and He gives us the account of Pharaoh in Genesis 41:25-57 to let us know to always be prepared. In this part of the Scripture, it tells us that Egypt will have seven years of abundance followed by seven years of famine. This was made known to Pharaoh by Joseph who was given such knowledge by God. Because Pharaoh was now aware of the coming famine, it would be foolish for him to ignore the warning and do nothing. However, Pharaoh was very wise, and he acted on Joseph's advice. When the famine came, Egypt endured. Had Pharaoh rejected Joseph's advice or waited until the famine came, his country would have collapsed. So, what is God trying to tell us here? He wants us to be wise and save during our good years to be ready for when we have bad years—which we *will* have. Because our job is still intact and we are still able to work, we ought to save now and not wait until something bad happens. Pharaoh had nothing to lose but everything to gain by saving. Whether the famine came or not, Pharaoh won either way.

Although 10% is what I suggest we save each month, God doesn't have a problem with us saving more than that. How do we know this? In Genesis 41:34, God said to Pharaoh through Joseph, *"Let Pharaoh appoint commissioners over the land to take a fifth of the harvest of Egypt during the seven years of abundance."* A fifth of the harvest is 20%. The Enemy will put thoughts into our minds telling us that a 20% savings rate is too hard to attain. But this is what Jesus said: *"With man this is impossible, but with God all things are possible"* (Matthew 19:26). So, who are we going to believe: God or Satan? Remember, the Serpent wanted Gideon to believe that he was the least in his family; but God said Gideon was a mighty warrior. Gideon chose to believe the Lord, and he was victorious.

A very important part of savings is having an emergency fund. The purpose of an emergency fund is to provide money for when there is a lack of income due to the loss of a job or unexpected high expenses like a car repair. Most financial planners recommend having enough money to cover at least three months' worth of expenses. For example, Jonadab's highest monthly cost of living is $3,400. Therefore, his emergency fund ought to have at least = ($3,400 x 3) = $10,200 in it. For many believers, however, this may not be feasible to do right away. Therefore, I suggest that you start by putting together a $1,000 emergency fund. Then, as your financial situation improves, put more money into your emergency fund until you have sufficient funds to cover at least three months of living expenses. Of course, it's always better to have a fund that covers a longer time frame than just three months. If you typically receive a tax refund, divert some or all of this money to establish your emergency fund right away. This step cannot be skipped, as it's extremely important. Also, money in an emergency fund should only be in a savings or money market account. The idea here is that you want to maintain the balance and be able to easily access the money should the need arise.

Earlier, I said to create a budget based on the highest monthly cost of living after considering at least six months' worth of spending. For any month in which the cost of living is less than the highest monthly cost of living, there will be extra money left over (once financial victory has been achieved, of course). Do not frivolously spend this money. Instead, divert the extra money into savings, use it to pay off debts, and/or put the money towards establishing an emergency fund. Remember, as His children, God wants us to always be prepared, but the Enemy wants us to do nothing until it's too late.

Financial Sacrifice Is Necessary

For us to save, invest, and have a better financial future, we must make financial sacrifices today. In His great love for us, God sent His only begotten Son, the Lord Jesus Christ, to come and die on the cross so that whosoever will believe in Him will have everlasting life. From Christ's sacrifice, God gave us the gift of eternal salvation. This means that when we go to sleep on this side of life, we get to wake up on the other side of life called Heaven. This was only made possible because of the sacrifice Christ made for us. It was only a one-time deal—that's it! Done. Finished!

God is not telling us to live off just eggs and Ramen noodles for our entire life just for the sake of trying to get victory in our financial health. God is only telling us to make some financial sacrifices. And from these financial sacrifices, we get a lifetime's victory in our financial health. That's it! Done. Finished! When we do this, we not only get to reap the fruits of our sacrifices, but we honor and glorify Him who enables us to get such victory. Deuteronomy 8:18 reminds us: *"...Remember the Lord your God, for it is he who gives you the ability to produce wealth."*

Financial sacrifice involves slashing some of our cost of living. Although this sounds simple, it isn't. The fight to conquer our desire to gratify ourselves now is one of the most difficult fights in the spiritual battle for our financial health. So, why is cutting costs difficult? Because our flesh wants to spend without restraint. Despite this, however, this fight is not impossible to win. Many of our fellow Christian brothers and sisters have already won this fight by taking up the sword of the Spirit and the armor of God and tapping into the power of the Holy Spirit. It can be done!

Proverbs 21:20 tells us, *"The wise store up choice food and olive oil, but fools gulp theirs down."* From a financial perspective, this verse encourages us to not spend everything we make and save. In other words, make financial sacrifices. We will use Jonadab's financial situation to illustrate how to go about doing this. We want to slash Jonadab's cost of living starting with his wants, followed by his debts, and then his needs. Again, the goal is to eventually get the income to be at least 10% higher than the cost of living after eliminating some costs. There are two ways we can do this: we can cut the cost of living to get to the income goal in one shot, or we can slash the cost of living gradually over time. Theoretically speaking, all his wants can be eliminated since none of these are required for Jonadab to live. If we did this, his income would immediately become = (($3,400 − $800)/$3,000) x 100% = 13.3% higher than his cost of living, and we would now accomplish our goal. But of course, this would be unrealistic. So let's try a different approach.

We'll cut $100 from his eat-outs, $300 from Jonadab's entertainment, do away with the $100 hobbies, and drop the cable and get only internet for $50, which yields a total savings of $550. This cost-cutting would cause Jonadab's income to be = (($3,400 − $550)/$3,000) x 100% = 5% higher than his cost of living, which is halfway to our 10% goal. To lower the cost of living further, we move onto the debt. We can get rid of his current car and replace it with a more affordable one. Now the new monthly auto loan payment becomes $150 and the auto insurance drops to $130, producing a savings of $220. Jonadab's income would then become = (($3,400 − $770)/$3,000) x 100% = 12.3% enabling us to achieve our goal.

Here's the point: No matter how we look at Jonadab's situation or our own financial situation, some sacrifices have to be made. Like I said, our flesh will fight against this. But we can win this fight. How? Because the "I am" who lives within us says so!

Increasing the Income Is a Must

At some point, cutting costs will no longer be possible. In fact, for some of us, cutting costs is not even an option at all. Therefore, increasing the income is the only viable avenue. I suggest cutting costs (if possible) and working on increasing the income simultaneously. No matter how it's done, the end goal is the same: The net monthly income must be at least 10% higher than the highest cost of living. There are four ways to raise the income:

1. Move up in one's current field of work
2. Go into a different career that pays more
3. Have others who are in the same household work
4. Start a business/side hustle with one's God-given gift

Unlike cutting costs, income has an unlimited upside potential. Therefore, the Devil will do everything in his power to prevent us from acting in this area of our finances. The Enemy knows that if we succeed in raising our income, he's finished. For this reason, he will use every lie at his disposal to stop us from acting on our income. One of the biggest lies the Enemy tells individuals here is, "You can't increase your income; it's too hard!" However, Philippians 4:13 says, "*I can do all this through him [Christ] who gives me strength!*" So, who are you going to believe: God or Satan?

Before moving up in your line of work, such as by taking on a supervisory role, it is good to evaluate yourself to ensure that you can do your current job well as God wants you to be promoted. Even if your work involves doing a lot of trivial things, do it with great care. Why? "*If you are faithful in little things, you will be faithful in large ones. But if you are dishonest in little things, you won't be honest with greater responsibilities*" (Luke 16:10 NLT). In addition, James 1:19 says, "*...Be quick to listen, slow to speak....*" To be a successful leader, you must develop a habit of listening rather than speaking, as it will help you to know more about what is going on in the area you have oversight in. Furthermore, as a supervisor, you will deal with difficult individuals sometimes. But remember: "*A hot-tempered person stirs up conflict, but the one who is patient calms a quarrel*" (Proverbs 15:18). One goal of a supervisor is to de-escalate difficult situations and not make them worse. These are just a few qualities to have to be successful in your move upwards.

Instead of climbing the ladder in one's current field, one could consider going into a completely new field altogether. This makes sense to do if your current field will not be able to provide the boost in income that you need to achieve financial victory, and the income of the new career far outweighs the cost of having to get additional education or training if required. For instance, let's say Ham makes $35,000 a year and has a total debt of $25,000. It doesn't make financial sense for him to pursue a job that pays $75,000 just to put himself into debt by another $100,000 due to the cost of training (for a total debt of $125,000)—but people do this. Hebrews 13:8 says, *"Jesus Christ is the same yesterday and today and forever."* What does this mean? It means that God's financial principles on how to manage money are also the same yesterday, today, and forever. Thus, if Ham can't manage his current income and smaller debt, making more money with even more debt will not suddenly make him a better money manager. Now, if the career change leads to a $75,000 salary and the cost of training is $10,000 or less, it would make financial sense for Ham to make the move. The whole idea is to get a higher-paying job without having to take on additional expenses or debts in the process.

It may be a good idea to also have others who are in the same household work (provided they are of age and able to work). The point of having more people under the same roof work is to increase the household income, reduce the expense burden, and enable savings for not just one person but all parties. When everyone in the household works together, everyone wins. This is one of the best strategies to quickly achieve financial victory for all involved. Like Ecclesiastes 4:9-10 states: *"Two are better than one, because they have a good return for their labor: If either of them falls down, one can help the other up."* Remember, though Jesus was fully God and fully man, He did not do the work that God the Father gave to Him alone. While on the Earth, Jesus enlisted others, such as the twelve disciples, to help Him carry out the work the Father entrusted to Him. The truth is our God is not a God who works alone. The three persons of God—Father, Son, and Holy Spirit—are always working together as one.

According to Romans 12:6-8 and 1 Peter 4:10, every one of us has a gift from God and we are to use our gifts to serve others. One way to do this is to launch a business or side hustle. Although the purpose of a business or hustle is to make money, you should only concern yourself with serving others to the best of your God-given gift based on God's truths—and let Him worry about bringing in the income. Ever wonder why Jesus's ministry on Earth was so successful? Because He focused His "business" on serving the needs of others and not Himself. In Matthew 20:28, Jesus made it very clear that He came to serve and not to be served. But you might be thinking: "I don't have any talent." That's not true. Everyone has a gift because that's what the Bible says. If you don't have a talent, it's because you haven't found it or the Enemy is lying to you. Jeremiah 33:3 says, *"Call to me [the Lord] and I will answer you and tell you great and unsearchable things you do not know."* So pray to God and He will help you find your gift.

The whole point of increasing your income is so that you can have victory in your finances as quickly as possible. It is not so that you can increase your spending, which would cause you to step out of God's plan.

God Wants Us to Sleep Well at Night

What Satan wants is for us to do nothing to improve our financial health and thus be consumed by fear, panic, anxiety, and stress when we are hit with a loss of income and/or an unexpected huge expense. However, this is not what God desires for us; He wants us to sleep well at night no matter what happens. In Acts 12, it says Peter was arrested and put into prison by King Herod for preaching the good news of the Lord. On the night before Peter was put on trial, Acts 12:7 tells us, *"Suddenly an angel of the Lord appeared and a light shone in the cell. He struck Peter on the side and woke him up. 'Quick, get up!' he said, and the chains fell off Peter's wrists."* Although Peter knew that it was likely he was going to be executed the next day, he still didn't lose any sleep at all. Peter was not afraid, nor was he even concerned. In fact, Peter slept so comfortably that the angel who appeared had to wake him up. Why did he sleep so well? Because Peter was in God's plan. Either way, he wins. If Peter is let go, he goes back to preaching the Word; if he is executed, he is in the presence of the Lord forever.

Listen, God wants us to still have a good night's sleep even knowing that come tomorrow, our job could come to an end. In other words, God doesn't want us to be afraid when our job goes away. Whether we are let go from our job or our employment continues, we win either way because we are in God's plan. And because we are sleeping so well, God has to send angels to "wake us up" for better opportunities that He has lined up for us!

CHAPTER VII
THE TRUTH ABOUT DEBT

Is God Against Debt?

Proverbs 22:7 tells us, "*The rich rule over the poor, and the borrower is slave to the lender.*" With respect to our time, this means that the banks rule over those who borrow from them and the borrowers are slaves to the banks or debts. We need to understand something about this verse before we go any further. Nowhere in it does it say *not* to get into debt. In fact, nowhere in the entire Bible will we find a scripture or passage that tells us to get into debt or not. There are circumstances when it is necessary to take on debt. For example, most people, including Christians, have to take out mortgages to buy their homes or take out loans to fund their education because of the high costs of these things.

At the same time, just because the Bible doesn't say that we cannot borrow does not mean that we should foolishly take on debt either. The point of the matter is that God is not against debt. He is only against us being slaves to debt—that's why the Bible admonishes us about borrowing. If there is a debt that the Bible encourages, it is the debt to love people.

Romans 13:8 says, "*Let no debt remain outstanding, except the continuing debt to love one another, for whoever loves others has fulfilled the law.*"

When we do borrow money, however, God expects us to repay (or make efforts to repay) what we borrow on time. That is why Romans 13:7 says, "*Give to everyone what you owe them: If you owe taxes, pay taxes; if revenue, then revenue; if respect, then respect; if honor, then honor.*" If we are unable to pay back money that is lent to us, we probably should not borrow any of it in the first place. In addition, borrowing money and purposely not repaying, if we can, is wrong (Psalm 37:21) and would be considered stealing, which would then violate the commandment to not steal (Exodus 20:15). So although debt itself is not a sin, it can lead to sin.

There are times when life happens, such as with the death of a spouse who is the breadwinner or the loss of a job, which can lead to financial hardship or struggle. In such scenarios, debts can suddenly become a problem. In some instances, it may even be impossible to pay back the debt or debts owed due to the reduction in income. Because our God is a God of love and mercy, He does not prohibit the use of bankruptcy to discharge debts in extenuating circumstances. We know this to be true because Matthew 18:23-27 tells us, "*...A king... wanted to settle accounts with his servants. As he began the settlement, a man who owed him ten thousand bags of gold was brought to him. Since he was not able to pay, the master ordered that he and his wife and his children and all that he had to be sold to repay the debt. At this, the servant fell on his knees before him. 'Be patient with me,' he begged, 'and I will* *pay back everything.' The servant's master took pity on him, canceled the debt, and let him go."*

Of course, the passage above isn't suggesting in any way that Christians should get into debt and then resort to bankruptcy as a means of escaping their debt obligations. This would be considered foolishness and willfully going against God. Nevertheless, it is still unwise to fall into debt bondage for these reasons:

- It can be very difficult to get out of debt depending on one's income relative to their expense and/or debt. The higher the debt relative to the income, the harder it will be to pay down or pay off the debt.
- The bankruptcy courts do not have anywhere near the same level of compassion and mercy as God. Not all debts will or can be discharged via bankruptcy (e.g., student loans, unpaid child support, alimony obligation, or taxes owed).

The bottom line is that God doesn't want any of us to be a slave to debt. If we want to be the masters of our debts (instead of our debts being our masters), there is only one way to do that: Stay in God's plan.

The Enemy's Debt Trap

The four most common debts in the U.S. are mortgage, student loan, auto loan, and credit card debt. Nearly every household has at least one or more of these debts. As I previously said, because we live in a fallen world, nothing is free—this includes borrowing money as well. Most kinds of debts or loans come with a cost called interest. This is what the banks charge us for borrowing money from them. If left unpaid, or if payment on a debt is insufficient, the interest on the debt will cause the balance to balloon over time, making the debt more and more difficult (if not impossible) to repay or pay off. The focus here is to help us stay in God's plan so that we don't become slaves to debt, as we already know that debt is a major problem and can hinder us from doing the will of God and cause problems in our own lives.

Remember, the flesh desires to spend without boundaries and the Enemy exploits this weakness to deceive us into debt bondage. One of the easiest ways for the Devil to get us addicted to spending and put us on the path toward debt slavery is through credit cards. How? Because they are very easy to get and most banks offer low-limit credit cards (e.g., $500 limit) for those who are new to using credit or have poor financial history. The idea of the Serpent isn't always to get us to immediately take on a large debt like a $40,000 car loan or a $100,000 student loan. No. There is a reason why he's called the Great Deceiver. Remember, the Enemy exercises absolute subtlety in everything he does to keep us completely oblivious to his vile schemes to destroy us financially.

By way of his lies via credit card advertisements, Satan plants thoughts into our minds to get us to apply for these low-limit credit cards—thereby setting us up for his debt trap. The Serpent wants us to believe that the low limit will prevent us from overspending. But the truth is that the Enemy plans to use these low-limit credit cards to get us to become addicted to spending. When it comes to credit cards, it's not "how much credit is available" that is the problem; it's always the spending part that gets us into financial trouble.

We are created beings with a free will. Thus, we ultimately decide whether to spend the credits that are on our credit cards or not. Remember Adam and Eve? They ultimately chose to go against God's command to not eat from the Tree of Knowledge, even though it was the Serpent who tricked them to do so. Once we develop that spending addiction or impulse, Satan can then easily steer us on the path to borrowing and spending more than what we make, leading us into debt bondage.

Now, I am by no means saying that we should not have credit cards. They do have their purpose and utility. For example, credit cards help us to build our creditworthiness and facilitate financial transactions, thus making purchasing things a whole lot easier—especially in today's world where e-commerce has become commonplace. In Chapter II, I said money is neither evil nor sinful; the same is true of credit cards. In addition, God is not against credit cards either.

So, when can we have or use credit cards? When we develop the financial discipline to restrain ourselves from overspending and have money to pay back what we spend in full each month. That is why I stressed the importance of budgeting, sacrificing, savings, and increasing our income in the previous chapter. By doing these things and making them a routine in our financial life, we not only develop financial discipline, but we will then also have the money to sufficiently cover our credit card payments and keep ourselves from falling into the Enemy's debt trap.

Getting Out of Debt Isn't Easy

Hosea 4:6 tells us, "*My people [believers] are destroyed for lack of knowledge.*" When we lack financial knowledge and wisdom, we are giving the Evil One the upper hand in our financial life in the sense that he can easily deceive us into taking on unnecessary and worthless debts.

The Enemy will try to get us to believe that we can always refinance or consolidate our debts if they ever get too burdensome. In refinancing, the idea is to obtain a new loan with a lower rate or longer-term length to pay off the current loan. Then, the borrower would pay off the new loan instead. In consolidation, a person takes out a single loan with a lower interest to pay off multiple higher-interest debts (typically credit cards). Then, the individual would in turn focus on paying just the consolidated loan that was used to pay off those multiple debts. On the surface, refinance and consolidation appear to be attractive ways to help people who are struggling to get a handle on their debts. However, those who are in deep debt and have trouble making payments on time will not qualify for favorable terms when it comes to refinancing and consolidating their debts because of their low credit scores. In addition, debt refinances and debt consolidation programs can be breeding grounds for scams.

Not only that, but Satan will even go to the extent of getting us to believe that financial advisors possess a magic bullet that will miraculously make our debts go away and that there are loan forgiveness and income-based repayment programs available to help us—just to lure us into debt slavery. Unfortunately, there is no such thing as a 100% debt eliminator tool or program that is simple or costs nothing as the Serpent wants us to believe. If there was such a thing, nobody would be in debt and all financial advisors would be rich. Loan forgiveness does exist, but it's only for debts like federal student loans. But even with student loan forgiveness being available, much less than 1% of all eligible borrowers will qualify for forgiveness. If this was not true, the U.S. would not have a nearly $2 trillion student loan debt crisis.

What about methods of dealing with debts, like the snowball and avalanche strategies? Both of these techniques are good debt management tools. The snowball method helps us to get rid of the smallest debt we have first regardless of the interest rate. Once we eliminate this debt, we move on to the next smallest debt. The avalanche technique, on the other hand, is used to eliminate the debt with the highest interest first. Again, once we finish paying off this debt, we tackle the next highest-interest debt. However, for both the snowball and avalanche methods to work, we must have extra money to put towards the debt that we choose to attack first. In other words, we must put more money into the debt we decide to take on first and continue to make the minimum payments on our other debts. Another drawback of these two methods is that they cannot be used to tackle debts that are significantly large, like mortgages and very high student loans.

Earlier I talked about bankruptcy and said that God is not against it. Nevertheless, not all debts will or can be discharged through bankruptcy. In addition, to file for bankruptcy, the struggling individual must show they lack the means to pay their debts, and the laws and rules on this differ from state to state. Satan wants us to believe we can easily use bankruptcy to relieve us of all our debts. Unfortunately, that is not the way bankruptcy works. If bankruptcy was such a simple and easy way to eliminate debts, nobody would be in debt. Furthermore, having a record of bankruptcy will impact one's ability to receive favorable borrowing terms for up to ten years or more depending on the situation. Moreover, bankruptcy can detrimentally affect an individual's job prospects as well because many employers look into this during their background checks.

So, what am I trying to convey here? I am saying that all methods of debt management have limitations. Depending on an individual's debt level relative to their income, the aforementioned methods may or may not be of help. This is something very important to keep in mind when taking on any kind of debt.

To illustrate the difficulty of dealing with debts, I will use three different student loan balances as examples for Jonadab: $20,000; $100,000; and $200,000. For the sake of simplicity, let's say the interest rate is 5% and applies to all three loan scenarios. Jonadab's monthly net income is $3,000. The following is a summary of each student loan situation:

Loan balance:	$20,000	$100,000	$200,000
Term length:	10 years	10 years	10 years
Interest rate:	5%	5%	5%
Monthly payment:	$212.13	$1,060.66	$2,121.31
% of net monthly income:	7.0%	35.1%	70.3%

Usually, student loans are to be paid off in ten years. As we can see just by looking at the figures, Jonadab would have an incredibly difficult time paying for a student loan of $100,000 or $200,000 with his current income, as the debt accounts for 35.1% or 70.3% of his net monthly income. And we haven't even accounted for his other expenses, such as monthly mortgage or rent, groceries, utilities, health insurance, and auto insurance. The point here is to simply show that the larger the debt relative to a person's income, the more difficult it will be to deal with it.

It is incredibly easy to rack up $100,000 debt. Unfortunately, the same cannot be said about trying to get a $100,000 salary, as these jobs are far and few between. It's important to understand that financial difficulty is not just a problem for someone who makes $3,000 a month. Even a person who takes home $15,000 a month can also experience financial distress if their debt or cost of living is much greater than their income. Individuals who fall into the latter situation are called HENRYs—High Earners, Not Rich Yet.

The Evil One is the father of lies. He will lie his way into our minds to get us to become addicted to spending. It is in our best interest to stay in God's plan because He doesn't want any of us to suffer from the trouble and pain that debt brings. In addition, being a slave to debt greatly hinders our ability to invest and grow the money God entrusted to us.

Understanding Net Worth, Assets, and Liabilities

So, when does it make financial sense to get into debt? Before I address this, we first need to understand the concepts of net worth, assets, and liabilities. Net worth is the total monetary value of an individual's assets minus all their liabilities; mathematically, net worth = assets - liabilities. What we are doing is totaling up the dollar amounts or worth of all our assets and liabilities, respectively. Then, we subtract our liabilities from our assets to arrive at our net worth. When it comes to net worth, it's either positive or not. The more positive or higher our net worth, the better.

In the previous chapter, I said that all money belongs to God and that we are simply just stewards of His money. Keeping this in mind, an asset is something that never wastes God's money because it brings in income and/or increases in value over time without us doing anything (excluding our savings, which requires that we put money away to increase it). Assets are things like jobs, rental properties, homes, savings accounts, stocks, and bonds. Jobs, rental properties, and bonds are income-producing assets. Rental properties, homes, and stocks build equity for us because they go up in value and can be sold for gains. Our assets serve two purposes:
1. Lump sum investing—where a large amount of saved money (e.g., $20,000) can be invested all at once.
2. Dollar cost averaging investing—where a specific amount of money (e.g., $100) from our income-producing assets (usually our job) is set aside to be invested periodically (e.g., bi-weekly or monthly).

Ecclesiastes 10:14 NLT tells us, *"No one [except God] knows what is going to happen; no one can predict the future."* That is why the Bible encourages us to save and invest wisely to be prepared. Thus, acquiring assets is very important to our overall financial health because it helps us build up our net worth. If we get our net monthly income to be greater than our highest cost of living (as previously discussed), we will automatically push our net worth into positive territory and increase our net worth over time. How? Because the money that's left over after accounting for our cost of living goes towards our savings. From here, money can then be distributed into investments like stocks and bonds.

Liability, on the other hand, is something that always wastes God's money since it takes money out of our pocket and/or decreases in value over time on its own. There are two kinds of liabilities: debts and things. Examples of debts are mortgages, student loans, credit card debts, and auto loans; examples of things are cars, TVs, and sofas. All debts take money out of our pocket, and things like automobiles, TVs, and sofas decrease in value and typically cannot be resold to recoup their original costs.

Even though the word "debt" has a negative connotation, not all debts are bad. For example, taking on debts is sometimes necessary to acquire assets like rental property and a home. In both of these situations, the debts are good because the rental property enables us to generate income. Additionally, the rental property usually goes up in value (like a home) over time. Thus, these debts are considered to be good debts. However, if we use the debts to purchase things like TVs and/or sofas, then the debts are considered bad because the items procured neither produce income nor increase in value. One of the purposes of the Devil is to get us to take on as many bad debts as he can.

I want us to understand something: God never said we are not to put money into liabilities like TVs, sofas, and vacations. In addition, God Himself isn't against us buying these things or enjoying the money He entrusted us with either. That's why Ecclesiastes 9:7-8 NLT tells us, *"So go ahead. Eat your food with joy, and drink your wine with a happy heart, for God approves of this! Wear fine clothes, with a splash of cologne!"* Our God is not a poor or cheap God. He is a God of infinite abundance, and He wants us to enjoy life. However, in Ecclesiastes 3:1 God says, *"There is a time for everything, and a season for every activity under the heaven."* In other words, God is telling us that the only time we should get into liabilities that take money out of our pocket and/or decrease in value is when our income is much greater than our cost of living. Not only that, but the liabilities we take on should never cause our cost of living to equal or exceed our income.

We have to understand that when we enjoy the money God gives us, we do it for His honor and His glory—not ourselves. We must know it's not in God's will for us to go broke or become poor while we enjoy life. Jesus came to Earth and did what He did so that all who come to Him may have life and have it abundantly (John 10:10), and this includes our financial life as well.

When It Makes Financial Sense to Take on Debt

Now that we know what net worth, assets, and liabilities are, I will address the question of when it makes financial sense to take on debts. We know that acquiring assets is super important for our financial health and using debts to acquire assets

is sometimes necessary. Having said this, a debt must satisfy the following four criteria before it can be considered worthy to have:
1. A debt must be used to procure an asset (except in a few cases, such as buying a car).
2. The asset acquired must generate income and that income must be more than enough to repay the loan.
3. The debt must not jeopardize the needs of the person.
4. The asset acquired increases in value over time on its own without the individual doing anything.

At the very least, the debt in consideration must satisfy criteria one, two, and three or one, three, and four. For example, Rachel took out $15,000 in student loans for her education, owes $6,000 on her car, and currently makes $60,000 a year after graduating. Jacob, however, downed $60,000 or 20% on a $300,000 home and borrowed $240,000 to cover the difference. In Rachel's situation, her student debt led to an asset (her job) which produces an income that is more than enough for Rachel to pay back the money she borrowed for her education and car. Thus, the debts she took on are unlikely to negatively impact her needs.

In Jacob's case, if he plans on living in the house he bought, it will not generate income for him to repay his debt. However, it's obvious Jacob has a stable and good-paying job. That's why he was able to put down 20% and secure a mortgage to purchase his home. In addition, real estate typically increases in value over time (despite even the worst housing crash like that of 2008), and thus, Jacob would eventually have equity in the home he bought. In fact, as of this book's publication, the values of U.S. homes are at their highest ever in history. As such, Jacob could unload his mortgage by selling the home to repay all of it should the need arise. Of course, Jacob could also rent out the home (in whatever manner he chooses) to bring in extra income to help pay for the mortgage if he so desires. Thus, his needs are unlikely to suffer from him taking on a mortgage.

On the other side of the debt spectrum, we have Athaliah, who makes $50,000 a year with only $500 in savings. She decides to take out a $40,000 auto loan. Then we have Japheth, who borrowed $100,000 to fund his education and now earns $25,000 a year after having finished school. In the case of Athaliah, her car is not an asset in the sense that it does not produce income. Thus, it will not help her repay her auto loan. In addition, automobiles typically decline in worth over time. Therefore, the vehicle will not build equity for Athaliah. In the event Athaliah suddenly loses her job and is unable to secure another job that would enable her to continue paying for her car loan, the bank could confiscate her vehicle for failure to meet her debt obligation. What's worse, Athaliah's overall well-being (not just her needs) would be detrimentally impacted by the sudden loss of her job and lack of savings. A car is a necessity and taking out a loan to buy one is fine. However, going broke over it is just pure foolishness.

In Japheth's circumstance, his education was unable to secure him an income that would allow him to repay his student loan. Unless Japheth can increase his income significantly, he will very likely be in debt bondage for a very long time. For Japheth to pay off his student loan in the typical ten years, he would have to fork over $1,000 a month (which won't be easy). Like Athaliah, Japheth's overall wellness is in jeopardy. As I said before, student loans are incredibly difficult to get discharged through bankruptcy because the courts have little to zero compassion and mercy for individuals who are in this situation. In addition, extremely few borrowers receive student debt forgiveness despite the program's good intentions. Assuming his student loans are federal, Japheth could apply for an income-based repayment option to help ease his debt payment burden.

Proverbs 22:7 tells us, *"...The borrower is a slave to the lender [or debt]."* This is always true with bad debts, but never with good debts. Why? Because good debts always pay for themselves. In both Rachel and Jacob's situations, their debts led to assets that enabled them to repay their debts. In the cases of Athaliah and Japheth, the debts they took on did not lead to assets that would help them to pay back the money they borrowed. As the prince of the air and the ruler of this world, Satan is constantly working to put us into the same predicament as Athaliah and Japheth. That's why so many advertisements we see out there only lead us down the path to debt bondage. Their sole purpose is to get us to spend and keep spending on things that don't generate income or only decrease in value. If this wasn't true, we would not have a debt crisis in America as well as within the Christian community.

Only the Word of God truly wants us to have victory in our finances. That's why Jesus said, *"I am the way and the truth and the life"* in John 14:6.

CHAPTER VIII
KINGDOM PRINCIPLES TO INVESTING—PART ONE

Wisdom Is Supreme

There are thousands of investment products to choose from in the world of investing. But why are there so many products out there? The answer is simple: The Enemy wants to mask the investments that have the most realistic chance to build wealth with those that do not. He does this to keep us confused, guessing, in fear, and financially poor. The Devil knows that Christians who become financially strong and obey the Word of God are a threat to his plan to enslave humanity. When followers of God lack financial knowledge and wisdom, they do not invest. Thus, they miss out on investments that have a high chance of growing their money. As a result, they are unable to build wealth. On the other hand, if they do invest, they end up putting money into products that have a low probability of actually growing their money. Why? Because the truth is there are far more investments that will not build wealth than those that can.

Even though the financial markets are already saturated with products that are unlikely to make money for most investors, more of these products continue to be created every year. Take cryptocurrency coins for example. There are over 20,000 of them in circulation since Bitcoin was first introduced in 2009. As of early December 2023, both Bitcoin and Ethereum (the top two virtual currencies) comprise about 70% of the $1.6 trillion total market capitalization of all cryptos. Despite their growing numbers, over 99% of these digital currencies are highly unlikely to create wealth for the vast number of investors. Although Bitcoin and Ethereum have climbed significantly relative to their values at their inceptions, their upward movements have been quite a rollercoaster ride. Because of their high volatility (the rapid rise and fall in value), it won't be easy to build wealth exclusively off of just these two—or any other—digital currencies.

Throughout this book, I have made a continual point to keep revisiting the subject matter of knowledge and wisdom, and now we know why. Knowledge and wisdom are required to discern which investments can realistically grow the money God entrusted to each of us. When we lack the ability to apply financial information, we are essentially giving Satan the upper hand against us when it comes to investing. This is why the Bible continually exhorts us to increase our knowledge and wisdom as we grow and mature in the faith. The belt of truth requires that we, as Christians, seek out God's truths always. Again, why? Because all the other pieces of the armor of God are dependent on the truth. Knowing the Word of God, which includes His financial truths, is a must for all of the other pieces of God's spiritual armor to work effectively against the deceptions and lies of the Evil One. Remember, God has a vested interest in our financial health because it's His money that we have!

Wisdom is so important—not just in the management of our finances. It is crucial to have wisdom to be successful in every area of our life. Because of its great significance, King Solomon asked God to give him the wisdom needed to govern the United Kingdom of Israel. In doing so, Solomon's reputation as the wisest king spread across the world of that time, making everyone want to come and see him. Many who came brought money and gifts to Solomon, which increased his wealth greatly. In 1 Kings 3:16-28, Solomon was put in a situation where he had to determine which of two women was the real mother of a baby. Because of his great wisdom, he quickly formulated a solution to solve the dilemma by having the child cut in half so that each woman could have half of the baby. In doing so, Solomon was able to find out who the real mother was (the one who didn't want the baby to be cut in half, of course).

The moral of this story is that wisdom enables Solomon to discern the truth from the lie. If Solomon needed wisdom to help him decide which of the two women was telling the truth or lying, why would we think that we don't need wisdom to help us discern which investments out of the thousands can grow our money? In this day and age where so many investment products are flooding the financial markets, it would be foolish to reject knowledge and wisdom. A lack of the right knowledge and wisdom in finance and investing is how people get into trouble when it comes to trying to grow their money.

Investing with a Purpose

Our God is a God of purpose. There is nothing He does that has no purpose. Therefore, when we approach investing, we, too, must do so with a purpose. One great example of God's purpose can be found in the story of Esther, a Jewish woman whom the Lord enabled to become the queen of King Xerxes of the Persian empire. In this account, an Agagite man named Haman, who was likely a descendant of King Agag of the Amalekites, was elevated by the Persian king to be the second most powerful official in his empire. When Mordecai, who was the cousin of Queen Esther, refused to pay respect to Haman, the latter was filled with much anger—especially because Haman had learned that Mordecai was a Jew. Because of Mordecai's lack of respect for him, Haman deceived King Xerxes into putting forth an irrevocable law that made it legal to exterminate all Jews in the Persian empire. With the help of Esther, however, Haman's plot to kill the Jews was ultimately thwarted and Haman himself was killed by order of the king.

What was God's purpose for Esther in all of this? The Jewish people in King Xerxes's kingdom were exiles from the Kingdom of Judah, which was made up of two of the twelve tribes of Israel: Judah and Benjamin. Both Mordecai and Esther were from the tribe of Benjamin. In 2 Samuel 7:16, God promised King David, who was of the tribe of Judah, that his house and kingship would endure forever through Jesus Christ the Messiah, who would eventually come from his lineage. This promise was originally made to Abraham, King David's forefather, by God in Genesis 12:3 when He said all people on Earth will be blessed through him. Satan was working around the clock in the heart of Haman to have all of the exiled Jews in the Persian empire eradicated in a single day. But God purposefully placed Esther in a position of influence to ensure that the covenant He originally made with Abraham (and later with David) remained intact so that Christ the Savior had a way to come into the world to redeem mankind and reconcile us back to God.

Hence, we should not approach investing haphazardly, but with a purpose—God's purpose that is. Investing is such a crucial part of the spiritual battle for our financial health that the Serpent does not want us to succeed. Satan knows that if we win here, we ultimately win the war. So, what is God's purpose for us here? To build wealth through investing wisely so that we can:
- Better carry on the work the Lord Jesus Christ called us to do—to go and make disciples of all nations and teach them to obey everything that He has taught us (Matthew 28:19-20)
- Be a blessing to others (Matthew 5:42) by providing them with financial support and/or imparting financial knowledge and wisdom to them
- Live a life of abundance in both the supernatural and the natural (John 10:10, 3 John 2) according to His truths.

Isaiah 55:8-9 tells us, *"'For my thoughts are not your thoughts, neither are your ways my ways,' declares the Lord.*

'As the heavens are higher than the earth, so are my ways higher than your ways and my thoughts than your thoughts.'" Since His ways are better than ours, we know that we can depend on Him completely, for He will never fail us. By being guided by His divine purpose, our mind will be focused on what the Spirit desires, thus keeping us in the plan of the Lord and safe from the Evil One.

Understanding Risk/Reward Is Critical to Building Wealth

As Christians before we embark on the road to invest the money that God entrusted to us, we must have a solid understanding of the relationship between risk and reward. Remember, there are thousands of investment products out there. To know which of these have the most realistic chance to build wealth, understanding risk and reward is a must. In investing, risk refers to the probability of losing money in an investment and reward refers to the potential financial gain from that same investment relative to its risk. Every investment product has its own unique risk as well as reward.

To have a clear understanding of risk and reward, we must first place all investments into one of two categories: traditional or alternative. Traditional investments refer to stocks, bonds, stock and bond funds (e.g., mutual, index, and exchange-traded funds [ETFs]), and money market accounts. All other investments are considered alternatives. Some common examples of alternative investments are commodities (e.g., gold, silver, oil, and corn), currencies (including cryptos and forex), venture capital/startups, private equities, pre-IPO placements, hedge funds, collectibles, non-fungible tokens (NFTs), and derivatives (e.g., futures and options).

Collectively as a group, alternative investments are far riskier than their traditional counterparts, but their potential rewards are also higher. What this means is that risk and reward have a direct relationship. In other words, the higher the risk, the higher the reward (or vice versa). However, what many investors—especially novices—fail to understand is that the higher the reward, the less likely it will be to get such a reward. The potential for no appreciable gain or loss is more probable. If this were not true, most people investing in mainly products of alternative investments would be rich. Now, I am by no means saying that individuals cannot build wealth by investing in alternative instruments. People have done it, so it is possible. Nevertheless, the truth is, in most cases, the odds of doing so are low. The greater risk associated with any alternative product is due to one or more of the following reasons (which I called anti-God characteristics):

- Lack of regulation
- Lack of transparency
- Lack of information to make informed decisions
- High-cost barrier to entry
- Lack of liquidity (i.e., difficult to buy or sell due to low number of participants and/or how its market/product is structured)
- High volatility (i.e., the prices or values of such investments can move up rapidly [due to hype, greed, or good news] or down sharply [because of dissipation of hype, bad news, or fear] at any time)

- Complex nature of the investments makes them difficult to understand
- Higher chance for fraud/scam due to one or more of the reasons given above

The listed risk factors is why financial experts do not recommend individuals to put more than 10% of their investing money into alternative investments. For most people desiring to build wealth, alternative investments would not be an appropriate strategy.

But it's quite obvious why alternative vehicles present such risk or instability. All the characteristics given above are contrary to God's nature, which is truth and balanced. Instability was a central theme throughout the Old Testament. When God's people, the Israelites, obeyed and revered Him, they experienced great stability and prosperity. However, when the people turned to evil and wickedness, strife and instability always followed. Because of this, the United Kingdom of Israel under the kingships of Saul, David, and Solomon eventually divided into two kingdoms: The Northern Kingdom of Israel and the Southern Kingdom of Judah. However, the deterioration didn't stop there. Ultimately, the sinful nature of both Israel and Judah led to their downfalls at the hands of the Assyrians and Babylonians, respectively, which effectively ended their monarchs and led to the demise of both Israelite kingdoms. King Josiah of Judah diligently tried to return to his kingdom to worship God, but his efforts were too late.

Although traditional investments have lower risks and lower rewards, this is only true when comparing them as a group with those of the alternative category. Within the traditional category itself, there is still significant risk/reward at play. The risk of loss is highest with stocks, moderate for bonds, and lowest with money market. Thus, stocks produce much higher returns than bonds and money market accounts. However, this doesn't mean that all stocks will deliver such gains. Since the whole point of investing is to grow our money, both bonds and money market accounts will not enable us to build wealth (at least not for most people anyways). Money market accounts pay between 0.01-5.0% APR depending on the bank and balance (most accounts pay at the low end of this range), and bonds pay rates of 3-6%. When inflation—which runs about 2-4% annually—and taxes are factored into the equation, the returns from money market accounts and bonds are significantly reduced or effectively become zero.

There are bonds called high-yield bonds or junk bonds that promise rates of 6-15%. However, these bonds are often offered by organizations or companies that are new, small, or in danger of default—hence the name "junk bond." Therefore, these bonds are not suitable for most investors. As such, this leaves us with just stocks and stock funds. Of all the asset classes, only stocks have a realistic chance to build wealth for most people over time for two main reasons:
1. Stocks increase in value over time with no upper limit.
2. The values of stocks are backed by work, which makes them reliable for building wealth.

Understanding Market Capitalization of Stocks

From an investing perspective, the best and easiest way to look at stocks is by market capitalization or market cap. Market cap

refers to the total value in dollars of a stock based on all of its outstanding shares. Stocks are divided into four groups according to the size of their market caps as follows:
- Micro-cap: < $250 million
- Small-cap: $250 million – $2 billion
- Mid-cap: $2 billion – $10 billion
- Large-cap: >$10 billion

In mathematical terms, market cap = stock price per share x number of outstanding shares. For example, the price of ABC stock is $100 per share and the stock has 80 million shares outstanding. Thus, the market cap of ABC stock is = ($100 x 80,000,000) = $8,000,000,000 or $8 billion, making it a mid-cap stock. Typically, the larger the market cap the larger the size of the companies of the stocks are as well. The opposite is true of companies with smaller-cap stocks. But what exactly does market cap tell us? It tells us where most investors' money is concentrated, which is good to know for successful stock investing.

Concerning market cap, stocks whose market caps are less than $2 billion are the riskiest. Nevertheless, these smaller market cap stocks also have higher reward potential. In terms of volatility, they, too, are the ones that experience the sharpest price climb or drop. For example, small-cap XYZ stock is trading for $5 per share with a market cap of $500 million. Its price can rise to $20 a share in just two weeks based on excellent news or just hype about the company's business. This would equate to = ($20/$5) x 100%) – 100% = 300% increase in XYZ's price or give the stock a new market cap of = ($20/$5) x $500 million = $2 billion. If Nadab invested $50,000 in XYZ stock, he would make a gain of = (($50,000/$5) x $20) − $50,000 = $150,000.

However, as enticing as the reward looks, the odds of Nadab reaping it are very low. The reasons for this? As of this book's publication, there are over 1,500 small-cap stocks and well over 10,000 micro-cap stocks. Trying to determine which of these stocks will deliver the type of gain like XYZ stock, when it will happen (which is not guaranteed to happen), and the exact time to get in and out to capture such reward won't be easy—even for professional investors and traders. Additionally, depending on the micro or small-cap stock of interest, it may not be so easy to buy or sell its shares due to the significant lack of liquidity. The illustration of small-cap XYZ stock from above sounds like the penny stocks I talked about back in Chapter II of this book. Indeed, small-cap stocks and penny stocks, which are also micro-cap stocks, tend to behave similarly. Of course, the Enemy will try to deceive Nadab into believing that he can easily become rich by investing in these small-cap stocks.

Scripture explicitly warns us in the first part of Proverbs 13:11 ESV that *"Wealth gain hastily will dwindle...."* Although it's possible to make a lot of money fast with micro and small-cap stocks, it's also a sure way to lose money fast. In actuality, this is exactly what happens to the vast number of people who try to make big and fast money from these smaller-cap stocks. From experience and analyses of historical price actions of stocks with market caps under $2 billion, the rapid rise in prices that the vast number of these stocks experience is short-lived and will decline very fast thereafter. Furthermore, when a person trades or invests in these smaller-cap stocks with real money, there are psychological and emotional biases that come into play that cause the individual, especially if they are new, to make irrational decisions resulting in losses.

The smaller cap stocks also exhibit some of the same anti-God characteristics that alternative investments have. Namely, they lack transparency, information, and liquidity. In addition, the regulation of penny stocks, which trade on over-the-counter (OTC) broker-dealer networks, is less stringent than stocks listed on major U.S. stock exchanges. Furthermore, micro and small-cap stock companies tend to have unproven or poor business models and lack loyal customers. Moreover, the smaller cap stocks have a higher chance for investment scams than the larger cap stocks (because there are less eyes on them).

For these stated reasons, investment advisors do not recommend allocating more than 10% of an investor's money to small-cap stocks. As for penny stocks, they are not appropriate for the vast majority of investors because of their inherent risk of significant losses.

On the other hand, we have large-cap stocks. The companies of these stocks tend to be large and many are well established in their respective industries. Together, these companies have a good history of gradual and sustained growth and value. Because of their lower volatility, it's very unlikely that we will see a 300% gain in a short time for these stocks (as I illustrated above with small-cap XYZ stock and DEF penny stock from Chapter II). Now, if we are talking about five years or longer, then a large-cap stock can jump 300% in its price or value. Of course, such a climb is not guaranteed to happen because we do not know the future. Unlike alternative investments, junk bonds, and stocks with market caps of less than $2 billion, large-cap stock companies usually are more transparent, have more information available for investors to make informed investment decisions, exhibit greater liquidity, and are less targeted by scams. These attributes, though imperfect, are more in line with God's character and the second part of Proverbs 13:11 ESV, which states that *"...whoever gathers little by little will increase it."* As such, large-cap stocks are the preferred stocks for investors to build wealth gradually.

As we now know, most investment products are not realistically viable options for building wealth because their traits conflict with God's nature, which makes them inherently unsound. Nevertheless, there is hope for building wealth in the small number of investments that display qualities that are reflective of God's truths and goodness.

The Importance of Work in Investments

When it comes to investments, work is very important because it's the work that's done behind the investments that creates real and sustainable values for investors. The principle of work is so important that God instituted it right from the beginning when He first created the Garden of Eden and then Adam and placed him in it to work (Genesis 2:7-8). Work wasn't something that man had to do because of sin. God intended man to work even before sin came into the world in Genesis 3:7. We know this to be true because Genesis 2:15

specifically tells us, *"The Lord God took the man and put him in the Garden of Eden to work it and take care of it."*

    Before I explain more about work, I want to first talk about what causes the price or value of an investment to increase or decrease, which will tie back to work. According to the principle of risk/reward, stock investing is the most realistic strategy for building wealth; therefore, I will focus mainly on stocks from here on out. So, what drives the price or value of a stock up or down? It is the buying or selling of shares in a stock by investors. When there is more buying than selling, the value of a stock rises. The opposite is true when there is more selling.

    But what factors cause investors to decide to get in or out of a stock? The major sources of influence on investors' buying or selling activities are wars, politics, pandemics, financial crises, economic news, inflation, interest rates, and company news and earnings. All of these factors will influence how investors think and feel about a stock or the stock market as a whole—and this is known as investor sentiment or belief. If overall sentiment is positive, buying will ensue, leading to an increase in the value of a stock or the market. If sentiment is negative, selling will occur, resulting in a decline instead. It is the rapid buying or selling of shares of stocks that leads to volatility (sharp climb or drop) in the market.

    Wars, pandemics, recessions, unsustainable economic expansions, and financial crises are viewed by investors as negatives; thus, when these things happen, selling is the typical reaction of investors. On the other hand, politics, economic information, inflation, interest rates, and company earnings can be interpreted by investors as good or bad depending on investors' perspective of the current state of the economy and/or the stocks of interest. Even what seemed like good news can be interpreted by investors as bad, and bad news can be seen as good. Whether market participants perceive the news as positive or negative, however, cannot be known in advance. Many financial experts and gurus will attempt to predict how certain stocks or the stock market will be impacted by these different factors. But the truth is that it's all just conjecture until it has come to pass. As Ecclesiastes 10:14 NLT reminds us, *"No one [except God] knows what is going to happen; no one can predict the future."*

Ultimately, if a Christian is investing for the long term (many years), all of what I just said above is irrelevant. Why? Because all of the factors I mentioned, except for economic information supporting stable economy and company earnings, have short-term influences (usually a few years or less than a year) on the rise and fall of stocks. For a stock, company earnings which shows or supports the ability of its company to generate revenues and ultimately realize profits from the sales of its products and/or services consistently is the key to creating real and sustainable value for investors of the stock over the long term. This is the work I am referring to, which will enable a stock to keep moving higher by attracting new investors (or new money) and keeping old ones. When new investors or money come in and current investors stay in the stock, the share price of the stock will rise and so will its market cap. For a new or small company, investors expect the revenue and net income to increase over time, which will then help the company expand. For a well-established company, revenue and net income are expected to be maintained if not rise over time.

When I say make money I am talking about profit, not revenue. A company realizes profit if its total expense, including taxes and interest payments for debts, is less than its revenue for the period in which the company reports its earnings (usually quarterly for publicly traded companies). The revenue is found at the top of a company's income statement, and the profit—which is the net income—is found at the bottom of the income statement. Regardless of what is going on in the economy or the world, if a company does not become profitable at some point, its stock price will go nowhere or spiral downward (unless investors believe the company will turn around). If a company continually loses money, it will eventually cease to exist. The old saying that profit is the lifeblood of a business is true.

The companies of large-cap stocks are the ones that typically have a track record of making money year after year from the sales of their products and/or services. This explains why most investors' money is concentrated in these stocks, and why they gradually increase in value over the long term—enabling investors of these stocks to slowly build wealth. Of course, some stocks can have market caps greater than $10 billion but their companies do not have histories of being profitable (as public companies), or the low earnings of the companies do not justify the high prices or values of their stocks. Examples of such stocks are IPOs, which are new stocks that just entered the market, and growth stocks, which have lots of investor money poured into them because of the belief that they will do well in the future. Regardless, always do research to make sure a company has a history of making money.

On the other hand, although the values of micro and small-cap stocks are backed by works from the sales of products and/or services, the vast number of companies of these stocks are unable to turn a profit, do not consistently make money, or are unable to increase their revenues and profits over time (despite positive sales). As for penny stocks, virtually all of these companies are not profitable. Investors who were in these smaller-cap stocks fled, and new investors tended to stay away as well. Thus, these stocks have less investor money concentrated in them as a group. This explains why the price jump in these stocks as I mentioned earlier is short lived or unstainable.

For comparison, the values of alternative products like cryptos, commodities, collectibles, NFTs, futures, and options are not backed by the kind of work I just discussed. With these products, the idea is to buy, hold, and hope that they increase in value. This hope is based on investor belief of what will happen in the future, which is called speculation. Thus, these investments are often called speculative investments. Of course, some (but not all) investors do analyze information such as economic data, historical prices, supply and demand metrics, future forecasts, and expert opinions to help them form their beliefs about the directions of the values of these investments.

Nevertheless, the analyzed information itself does not create value in the alternative investments mentioned above.

It's how much investors are ultimately willing to pay based on what they believe that gives these investment vehicles their market values. So long as investors continue to believe in these investments, the buying of these products will prevail and their values will climb. However, when they stop believing, the prices of the products will drop because selling will prevail—and this is the real danger of investing based on belief. From a biblical perspective, speculative investments are the equivalent of fantasies. That is why Proverbs 28:19 tells us, *"...Those who chase fantasies will have their fill of poverty."* With investments backed by work that produces profits, however, it's not a matter of belief. When a company is consistently and increasingly profitable over time, it automatically attracts investors.

In the world of investing, work that leads to profitability (as described) is what creates real value for investors of an investment. Likewise, in the world of faith, work resulting in good deeds is what creates a real relationship between God and believers. That is why James 2:17 ESV says, *"...Faith by itself if it does not have works [of good deeds], is dead."* The same can also be said about investing. Any investment that does not have work that produces profits is also dead.

CHAPTER IX
KINGDOM PRINCIPLES TO INVESTING—PART TWO

The Basics of the Stock Market

The knowledge gained from Chapter VIII about stocks is great. However, that information alone isn't enough to be a successful stock investor. This is akin to knowing how to pray but not knowing the Word of God. To get results from praying, Christians must know the will of God—that is, they must know the truth about God and the realms of the natural and supernatural. This is why when we pray for healing, deliverance, or change, nothing happens. Why? Because we don't know God's desire or plan, which has an expected outcome. However, when our desires align with God's desires because we know His will, we can then pray and expect to see results. This same principle applies to stock investing as well. When we know how the stock market works, then we can invest and expect to see results.

Therefore, before going forward, it's important to have a basic understanding of the U.S. stock market and the major stock indexes. The stock market is comprised of 11 sectors as follows:

Communication Services	Industrials
Consumer Discretionary	Information Technology
Consumer Staples	Materials
Energy	Real Estate
Financials	Utilities
Health Care	

Each sector is made up of two or more industries. Stocks are then placed in a certain industry or a sector based on their companies' business attributes. For example, Intuit (INTU) deals mainly with software-related products and services so its stock falls under the Software industry of the Information Technology sector.

There are many stock exchanges in the U.S. The two major stock exchanges are the New York Stock Exchange (NYSE) and the Nasdaq—both of which are located in New York City. As of this publication, there are about 2,300 stocks listed on the NYSE and over 3,600 on the Nasdaq. All companies listed on the NYSE or Nasdaq are public companies. Hence, their stocks are registered with and regulated by the U.S. Securities and Exchange Commission (SEC) to ensure investors' trust and confidence. NYSE and Nasdaq facilitate the buying and selling of stocks between parties. In addition, there is constant oversight and management of all these transactions.

Like stock exchanges, there are also many stock indexes. The three major U.S. stock indexes are the Dow Jones Industrial

Average (DJIA), S&P 500, and Nasdaq Composite. The purpose of these indexes is to give investors an overall picture of the financial health or performance of the stock market. The DJIA tracks 30 of the largest blue chip U.S. companies, which include Walmart (WMT), Disney (DIS), and Nike (NKE). All stocks on the DJIA have market caps greater than $10 billion. The fact that there are only 30 stocks on the DJIA makes this index an unreliable indicator of the health of the stock market. The DJIA is a price-weighted index; therefore, the number of points moving up or down on this index is heavily dictated by the stocks with higher prices. Those with lower stock prices do not influence the index's movement much even if the price movement of such stocks is significant percentage-wise. For example, when the price per share of WMT stock changes, it will have a greater impact on the DJIA's movement than Walgreen's (WBA) stock because of the former's higher stock price. As of early December 2023, WMT stock was trading for about $154 per share while WBA stock was going for $20 a share. Of the three major indexes, the DJIA is the least volatile.

The S&P 500 tracks 500 of the largest U.S. company stocks (mainly stocks with market caps greater than $10 billion). The S&P 500 is more diversified than both the DJIA and Nasdaq Composite indexes because it includes companies from various business industries, such as technology, healthcare, communications, financials, etc. Therefore, economists and the general public like to use the S&P 500 to gauge the general health of the stock market and the U.S. economy. Unlike the DJIA, the S&P 500 is a market cap-weighted index. In other words, the stocks with the bigger market caps will have more influence on the value of the index than those with smaller market caps. For instance, both Visa (V) stock and Bank of America (BAC) stock are tracked by the S&P 500. However, as of the beginning of December 2023, because the stock of V has a market cap of roughly $520 billion versus BAC's market value of about $240 billion, the price change in V will contribute more to the movement of the S&P 500 than that of BAC.

The Nasdaq Composite tracks more than 3,000 stocks. Half of the stocks on the Nasdaq Composite are technology and internet companies. Unlike the DJIA and S&P 500, the Nasdaq Composite not only holds large-cap stocks but includes stocks with market caps of less than $10 billion as well. For these two reasons, the Nasdaq Composite is the most volatile of the three major indexes. This means that when stocks do well or poorly, this index typically rises or falls the most compared to the other two indexes. For example, if the entire stock market jumps 2%, the Nasdaq Composite could be up 3%. On the other side, if the market is down by 2.5% this index could tank by 3.5%. Because it is mainly technology-heavy, it does not represent the overall picture of the stock market or the U.S. economy. Like the S&P 500, the stocks with the larger market caps are the ones with the greater influence driving the value of the index.

Over the long term, the DJIA, S&P 500, and Nasdaq Composite tend to move higher. Why is this so? Because stocks in the indexes can be removed or replaced if they fail to meet specific standards of the respective index. In other words, when a company of a stock is not profitable or is in serious legal trouble, its stock can be booted out of the index. If this were to occur, a better-performing stock meeting the standards of the specific index would take the place of the stock that was ejected. Many of the stocks tracked by the major benchmarks are backed by work that produces profits as discussed in the previous chapter. It is this process of removing and replacing stocks that helps to maintain the values of the indexes and push them higher in the long run—which is good to know to be a successful stock market investor and build wealth.

Diversification Is a Must

Something very important to understand about stock investing is that no stock, including even large-cap stocks, is immune from becoming worthless (no matter how good it is) and this can happen at any time without warning. Why? Behind every stock is a company and a company is run by people with a corrupt inclination called the flesh. Galatians 5:17 reminds us that "...*the flesh desires what is contrary to the Spirit, and the Spirit what is contrary to the flesh.*" That's why God explicitly instructs us in Ecclesiastes 11:2 to "*Invest in seven ventures, yes, in eight; [for] you do not know what disaster may come upon the land.*" In other words, diversification is an absolute must when it comes to investing (regardless of the investments) in a broken world such as ours.

Of all the kings and kingdoms of Solomon's time, he and his kingdom were the greatest (1 Kings 10:23) because of the great wisdom God had given to Solomon to rule and govern his people. Yet, despite his incredible wisdom, Solomon still sinned against God, and the United Kingdom of Israel under him did not last. The kingdom was immediately torn apart after Solomon died. Ten of the twelve tribes of Israel were given to Jeroboam, a subordinate and official who served under Solomon. Only the tribes of Judah and Benjamin remained with Rehoboam, the son of King Solomon, who succeeded him. Why did this happen? Because Solomon's mind was ruled by the desires of his flesh. Although he had a wife, Solomon's flesh loved and desired many foreign women—women who were from nations that God explicitly forbade Israelite men to marry because He knew they would turn the hearts of the Israelites away from the Lord. But the Bible tells us, *"Nevertheless, Solomon held fast to them in love. He had seven hundred wives of royal birth... and his wives led him astray"* (1 Kings 11:2-3). Because he placed his desires above God's (which was due to his pride), Solomon fell from the Lord's favor, and his kingdom was doomed from that point on.

Despite Solomon's amazing wisdom, without God, he was no match for Satan's influence over his mind. In Solomon's situation, he had three forces working against him: Satan's lies (in the forms of voices and whispers in Solomon's mind), the lust of his flesh (which desired the foreign women), and the influences (e.g., spoken words and appearances) of the foreign women and those already married to Solomon (who were also under the powers of the Evil One). As the prince of the air, the Enemy knew just how wise Solomon was through his observations of the king. Thus, the Serpent made sure to increase Solomon's fleshly cravings for the foreign women with his lies, thereby causing Solomon to ultimately take 700 of them to be his wives. In doing so, Solomon only strengthened the

Enemy's stronghold over him. Since his mind was so polluted with lustful and worldly thoughts, he was completely oblivious to the deceptions of Satan, who was working 24/7 in the hearts of his wives to turn Solomon and his kingdom away from God and towards wickedness and idol worshiping.

Solomon was the wisest person of his time. Yet, he still fell. If such a man of Solomon's caliber could fall, why would we think even for a second that the best stock or stocks in the world cannot fall? Although stocks are not people, the companies behind them are run by people. And Scripture makes it very clear in Romans 3:10 and 12 that *"There is no one righteous, not even one. All have turned away...."* Further, Romans 3:23 says, *"...All have sinned and fall short of the glory of God."* The words *"no one"* and *"all"* in these verses include every person, including Solomon, who has ever lived or will live. The Word of God is so true. Back in 2000, American conglomerate General Electric (GE) had a market cap of over $500 billion and was the world's most valuable company and stock. Despite its position as the number one company and stock on the planet, GE was still not immune to the same fate as Solomon. The company's pride, a series of foolish financial and business decisions, and misleading investors and regulators caused it to lose money, trust, and ultimately over 80% of its stock value by mid-2020. By then, GE's market cap fell to $40 billion—or less than a tenth of what it was at its highest valuation in history. Because of the company stock's lackluster performance, the stock was removed from the DJIA and replaced with WBA. (As of February 26, 2024, WBA has been replaced by Amazon [AMZN] as its company failed to perform.)

Stocks that were once gems to investors that ceased to exist, included Enron (ENE) and WorldCom (WCOM). ENE was an energy and utility company, and WCOM was the second-largest telecommunication provider in the U.S. at its height. These two companies committed two of the largest financial and accounting scandals in U.S. history in the early 2000s. As a result, their stocks were quickly wiped out. The Bible repeatedly reminds us of one truth: A mind that is governed by the flesh always falls. Why? Because the person is easily influenced by the Enemy's lies to carry out the desires of their flesh. In the cases of ENE and WCOM, they told investors they were making money when in actuality they weren't. Both companies thought they could keep faking it until somehow things got better. But Proverbs 10:9 clearly says, *"Whoever walks in integrity walks securely, but whoever takes crooked paths will be found out."*

At their peaks, both ENE and WCOM had market caps of $70 billion and $180 billion, respectively, which indicated to the public that these two companies were among the most transparent corporations on the planet. Yet, fraud was still found in them. What does this tell us? Fraud is a choice. This is what makes investing in a single stock or any single investment dangerous. Anyone who had their entire life's savings in GE, ENE, or WCOM would have been completely and financially ruined.

Due to the risks associated with single stocks, we must diversify—which leads me to the discussion of stock funds.

Understanding Stock Funds

There are three kinds of stock funds: stock mutual funds, stock index funds, and stock ETFs. A fund can hold as few as thirty stocks to over a hundred and can be a mixture of different market cap size stocks depending on their investment goals (e.g., growth, income, and/or stability). The purpose of these funds is to provide investors with diversification to prevent or minimize loss of money due to one or a few stocks not doing well. When a fund contains many stocks, it is less probable that all companies of these stocks will fail simultaneously. Just like the major U.S. stock indexes, stocks within stock funds are removed or replaced to ensure that the funds continue to meet their investment return objectives. Like single stocks, all stock funds must be registered with the SEC before the financial firms who operate them are allowed to sell shares of the funds to investors.

Below are key characteristics of the three different stock funds:

	Stock Mutual Funds
Goal:	Seek to get returns that are better than a benchmark like the DJIA, S&P500, or Nasdaq Composite
Management style:	Actively managed; stocks within these funds are frequently removed or replaced in attempt to beat a specific benchmark the fund is being compared to
Expense ratio:	0.50-1.50%
Upfront fees:	Front-end load (up to 8.5%) and/or back-load (usually 5%)

Stock Index Funds	
Goal:	Seek to mimic the returns of certain stock indexes like the DJIA, S&P500, or Nasdaq Composite
Management style:	Passively managed; once stocks are selected for the funds, no further stock picking or trading occurs (except for time-specific rebalancing)
Expense ratio:	0.10-0.50%
Upfront fees:	Most are no-load funds (no buying or selling fees)

Stock ETFs	
Goal:	Seek to mimic the returns of certain stock indexes like the DJIA, S&P500, or Nasdaq Composite or certain stock market sectors/ industries such as Energy or Health Care
Management style:	Most are passively managed; once stocks are selected for the funds, no further stock picking or trading occurs (except for time-specific rebalancing)
Expense ratio:	0.02-1.00%
Upfront fees:	Trading commission (varies depending on brokerage firm)

When deciding to invest in stock funds, there are four points that must be taken into consideration:
1. Management style of the funds
2. Cost of holding shares of the funds long term
3. Opportunity to buy or sell shares of the funds
4. Historical performances of the funds

With an actively managed stock mutual fund, there is no guarantee that it will do better than the market or the index it's trying to beat. The long-term average annualized return of the S&P 500 is 10-11%. For a fund to outperform the S&P 500 or whichever benchmark it's being measured against, a financial manager may need to employ riskier investment strategies (e.g., futures and options) to achieve a higher return. The riskier strategies, nonetheless, could backfire—resulting in losses instead. In fact, 80% of actively managed funds underperform. In addition, finding a financial manager who possesses the expertise and skills to beat whichever benchmark a fund is being compared to year after year won't be easy, since there are very few individuals with this kind of aptitude. Thus, finding a financial manager who can deliver high returns year after year is like trying to find a small-cap stock that will generate a 10,000% gain in a short period and then trying to capture all of that gain.

In a passively managed stock index fund or ETF, however, there is no active trading of stocks or management of the fund. Instead, the financial manager selects stocks from a stock index (such as the DJIA or S&P 500), or a particular market sector/industry and puts them into the index fund they are managing. The financial manager may pick a sample of stocks or all the stocks that make up the particular index or stock sector. The idea is to build a fund that simply replicates the movements and returns of a stock index or sector year after year. In most cases, a passively managed fund does better than its actively managed counterpart in terms of return over the long run with little to no effort on the part of the financial manager. Although stock index funds and ETFs tend to move similarly to the benchmarks they are attempting to mirror, the movements of the funds will not be exactly the same.

The costs associated with a stock fund can greatly reduce its return. Of the charges mentioned, the expense ratio is the most significant because it is ongoing. The expense ratio refers to a fund's annual operating expenses (or how much it costs to run the fund) and is expressed as a percentage. It is found by dividing the total operating expense by the fund's total assets and multiplying it by 100. The expense ratio includes administrative, management, advertising, and other operating costs. For example, an actively managed MNO stock mutual fund's annual operating expenses are $7 million and its total assets are $350 million. Thus, its expense ratio would be = ($7 million/$350 million) x 100 = 2%. As a rule of thumb, an expense ratio of less than 0.75% is considered reasonable. (Of course, the lower the better.)

If Darius plans to invest a lump sum of $1,000 into the MNO stock mutual fund, assuming an average annual rate of return of 15% over 30 years, his account (or future value) would be worth = present value x $(1 + \text{rate})^{\text{years}}$ = $1,000 x $(1 + 0.15)^{30}$ = $66,211.77 at the end of that time. But since MNO has a 2% expense ratio, Darius's actual yearly return is 13%, not the 15% quoted. Thus, his account would be valued at = $1,000 x (1 + 0.13)^{30} = $39,115.90. Over the 30-year time frame, however, Darius would have paid out = $66,211.77 − $39,115.90 = $27,095.87 in fees tied to the expense ratio. This cost is a whopping = ($27,095.87/$66,211.77) x 100 = 41% reduction in Darius's account value after 30 years of investing, which is significant. Below is a comparison between hypothetical MNO and STU stock funds at the end of a 30-year investment period for Darius:

	MNO stock mutual fund	STU stock ETF
Present value: (principal amount)	$1,000	$1,000
Rate of return: (average annualized)	15%	13.8%
Expense ratio:	2%	0.10%
Future value: (before expense ratio)	$66,211.77	$48,335.68
Future value: (after expense ratio)	$39,115.90	$46,077.56

As we can see, although MNO had a higher rate of return than STU, the latter made more money for Darius than the former after accounting for the expense ratio. Additionally, Darius pays the expense ratio fee whether a fund makes money for him or not. This is why it's so important to evaluate the cost of buying/owning stock fund shares because they can take a huge bite out of our returns over the long term. Therefore, just because a fund can deliver a high return doesn't necessarily mean that we will get to keep all of that gain because of the charges we have to pay. Of the three types of stock funds, most index funds and ETFs have lower expense ratios than mutual funds.

The third point that we need to consider is the opportunity we have to buy and sell the stock funds. With mutual funds and index funds, we can only buy or sell shares of these funds at the end of the close of the market. With ETFs, on the other hand, we can buy or sell their shares at any time when the stock market is open. Why is this important? Having more opportunities to buy or sell is critical to being able to keep as much gain as possible or prevent major losses. For example, if the stock market jumped 5% at noon time and Martha wanted to sell her ETF (which also climbed by 5.5%) to capture the big gain, she could do so immediately. On the other hand, if a piece of bad news surfaced and caused the market to tumble by 2%, Martha could decide to unload her ETF (which has dropped by 2.2%) right away to mitigate further losses should the bad news continue to weigh heavily on stocks in the days afterward.

Recall that I said the DJIA, S&P 500, and Nasdaq Composite typically move higher over the long run. When evaluating stock funds to invest in, always look at their historical performances to see if they have been moving in the same direction as the major indexes. We need to know this because not all funds will increase in value over time. Some funds—depending on how they are constructed or the sectors/industries they reflect—will fluctuate from year to year or over a period of years without actually climbing. Others may be in a downward trend. The gyration or downward movement in values of these funds may be due to what is going on in the economy and the world impacting those funds or the companies of the stocks in the funds not making money. The key here is to focus on funds that are trending in the same direction as the major benchmarks. Index funds and ETFs that are designed to specifically mirror the S&P 500 or another index will behave almost the same as that benchmark.

Although good past performances do not guarantee similar future performances (because the future is unknown to us), it is still wise that we check the past performances of stock funds of interest against the major indexes to give us an idea of whether the funds will continue to march higher or not. As I said, if a stock fund is designed to follow one of the major indexes, it most likely will perform similarly to that index into the future.

Long-Term, Diversified Investing Is the Key to Building Wealth

For the vast majority of people, including Christians, financial victory is not something that happens overnight or in just a few months. The same is true with building wealth—it is going to take time. But most importantly, willingness and obedience through faith will be the factors that will enable an individual to build, attain, and sustain their wealth. That is why

Isaiah 1:19 says, "*If you are willing and obedient, you will eat the good things of the land.*" When Joseph was appointed second-in-command of Egypt by Pharaoh, the nation of Egypt became the world economic powerhouse when famine eventually came over the lands. How do we know this? Genesis 41:57 tells us, "*...All the world came to Egypt to buy grain... because the famine was severe everywhere.*" The Egyptians were only able to "*eat the good things of the land*" because Pharaoh and his people were willing and obedient to the instructions given by God to Joseph.

Of course, Egypt becoming the ultimate economic center of the world at that time wasn't something that happened right away. During the seven years of abundance, the Egyptians had to consistently do their part, which was doing what was possible for them—that is, they collected the food, grains, and produce and stored them away. While the Egyptians did their part, God was doing His part, which was the impossible—that is, He greatly multiplied all the things they had stored or saved. We know this to be true because Genesis 41:49 says, "*Joseph stored up huge quantities of grain, like the sand of the sea; it was so much that he stopped keeping records because it was beyond measure.*" It was the Egyptians' willingness and obedience to God's truths that enabled them to reap the harvest of the land and made their country's economy the number one of that time.

So, how can Christians begin to build wealth? It's quite simple: Be willing and obedient through faith to Proverbs 13:11 ESV, which states, "*Wealth gained hastily will dwindle, but whoever gathers little by little will increase it*" and

Ecclesiastes 11:2, which says, *"Invest in seven ventures, yes, in eight; [for] you do not know what disaster may come upon the land."* In other words, stay focused on long-term investing and diversify one's position with stock funds containing mostly financially strong companies. Long-term investing is defined as holding a position for one year or longer.

The Parable of the Talents, which is found in Matthew 25:14-30, provides the key kingdom scriptures to building wealth and affirms what God also says in Proverbs 13:11 ESV and Ecclesiastes 11:2. In this parable, we have a master who was going away for a long time and gave five talents to one servant, two talents to a second servant, and one talent to a third servant (all according to their abilities). During biblical times, a talent was used as a unit of weight for valuable metals such as gold and silver. One talent of gold is roughly 1,200 ounces. As of the start of December 2023, the price of gold was about $2,000 per ounce. Therefore, the talents of gold in approximate U.S. dollars are as follows:

No. of Talents	Price of Gold/Ounce	Ounces of Gold	Talent Value
1	$2,000	1,200	$2.4 million
2	$2,000	1,200	$4.8 million
5	$2,000	1,200	$12 million

The servant with the five talents invested his portion and gained back five additional talents for a total of = $12 million x 2 = $24 million, and the one with two talents put his to work and got back two more talents for a total of = $4.8 million x 2 = $9.6 million. Ever wonder how the five and two-talent servants were each able to double their money or get a return of 100% on their investment? They did exactly what Proverbs 13:11 ESV and Ecclesiastes 11:2 instructed.

I will illustrate the financial truths of Proverbs 13:11 ESV and Ecclesiastes 11:2 using the S&P 500. Investors cannot invest in the S&P 500 directly. However, they can invest in index funds or ETFs which replicate this major U.S. stock index. Below is a summary of the gains for the servant with the five talents had he invested all five talents in the S&P 500 beginning in January 1993 and waited until June 2023:

S&P500			
Date	Price[a]	Investment Balance[b]	%Gain
January 1993	$440	$12 million	N/A
June 1997	$880	$24 million	100%
April 1999	$1320	$36 million	200%
October 2013	$1760	$48 million	300%
November 2016	$2200	$60 million	400%
November 2017	$2640	$72 million	500%
November 2019	$3080	$84 million	600%
August 2020	$3520	$96 million	700%
March 2021	$3960	$108 million	800%
June 2023	$4400	$120 million	900%

a: *Major stock indexes are reported in points, not dollars (but the points do represent dollars); the price of S&P500 when it climbed by $440 each time*
b: *Investment balance does not account for dividends and inflation*

From the illustration, we can see that the servant with five talents not only easily made 100% gain after four years of investing in the S&P 500, but he was able to increase his investment balance or principal by 900% by continuing to hold his position until June 2023—which lines up with what Proverbs 13:11 ESV says: *"...whoever gathers little by little will increase it."* Even though GE, ENE, and WCOM stocks were a part of the S&P 500, their downfall or demise did not hurt the servant's investment return at all. Why?

- The S&P 500 contains 500 stocks. Thus, it is well diversified against a few stocks like GE, ENE, and WCOM not doing well or being wiped out just as Ecclesiastes 11:2 warns us: *"Invest in seven ventures, yes, in eight; [for] you do not know what disaster may come upon the land."*
- As the market caps of GE, ENE, and WCOM decreased in value, these stocks also had less and less influence on the value of the S&P 500. Remember, the S&P 500 and Nasdaq Composite are market cap weighted. Stocks with bigger market caps have a greater impact on these two indexes than smaller cap stocks.
- ENE and WCOM were eventually removed from the S&P 500 and replaced with better-performing stocks.

Had the servant with the two talents invested in the S&P 500 during the same time, his percentage gains would've been the same as the servant with the five talents. In fact, all investors who invested a lump sum of money in the S&P 500 in January 1993 and allowed that money to sit until June 2023 saw the same percentage return.

Since its inception in 1957, the S&P 500 has had an upward trend to date. Additionally, the S&P 500 has low volatility (i.e., its values move up or down slowly) and high trading volumes (i.e., lots of buying and selling activity). Therefore, this makes it very easy for investors to sell their positions (assuming they could buy this index) when their investments have gains of 100% or more. Although the Bible does not explicitly state what the five and two-talent servants invested their talents in, they probably invested in something like the S&P 500 long term. This would explain how both servants, who worked for the same master, were able to easily double their talents and account for their gains when the master finally returned to settle accounts with them after a long time (Matthew 25:19-20, 22).

As for the servant given the one talent, he missed out on 900% of the gain (assuming the two servants who invested did so in the S&P 500 since January 1993 and held their positions until June 2023). The point is that when an individual lacks financial knowledge and wisdom, they do not invest; thus, they miss out on investments that have a high chance of growing their money.

CHAPTER X
KINGDOM PRINCIPLES TO INVESTING—PART THREE

Do Not Fear Stock Market Crashes

Whenever there is talk of a stock market crash, the spirit of fear takes hold of many investors as well as the general public. From a technical standpoint, a stock market crash occurs when it drops 20% or more from its most recent highest peak. What causes stock market crashes? Financial experts and economists like to tell us that wars, pandemics, financial crises, government instabilities, and inflation are the causes of stock crashes. But the truth is pride, foolishness, and ignorance of the flesh are the real causes of all stock market crashes to date. It is these fleshly traits that enable Satan to manipulate the minds of the world, triggering wars, financial crises, and instabilities.

When investors are overtaken by fear, they sell much of their stock holdings, causing a steep decline in the market leading to a stock crash. In some cases, like the U.S. stock market crash of 1929 (which was the worst crash in U.S. history) where the DJIA dropped nearly 90%, fear can exacerbate a crash by causing it to be worse than what was going on that brought on the crash. Many factors led to or fueled the 1929 stock crash: speculation, oversupply, poor government policies, lack of regulation, and excess debt—all of which were due to the pride, foolishness, and ignorance of the flesh. But it was the spirit of fear working in the minds of investors, banks, governments, and the public that caused people to overreact or respond inappropriately. This led to more instabilities in the financial and economic systems, triggering more stock selloffs. This, in turn, provided more fuel for the spirit of fear to be able to do more damage to the market than what was going on, which was exactly what the Enemy wanted.

After the stock market collapse of 1929, many Americans were awash in fear and were frightened to invest in the stock market again. Why was fear so strong in those who didn't want anything to do with the stock market? The account of the twelve Hebrew men sent by Moses (after the Israelites' exodus from Egypt) to explore Canaan, the land which God had promised to give to the Israelites, in Numbers 13 and 14 provides one of the best illustrations of how fear is greatly stirred up in people.

The chosen men went up to the Promised Land from Kadesh (where the Israelites camped) in the Desert of Paran. After scouting the land as instructed, they returned to the Israelite community and reported their observation: "*...The land... does flow with milk and honey! Here is its fruit. But the people who live there are powerful, and the cities are fortified and very large. We even saw descendants of Anak there [who* *were descendants of the Nephilim]"* (Numbers 13:27-28, 33). Although Caleb and Joshua, who were among the twelve men who explored Canaan, believed the Israelites could take the land, the other ten men did not. These men said to Moses and the Israelite assembly: *"...We can't attack those people [in Canaan], they are stronger than we are.... The land we explored devours those living in it. All the people we saw there were of great size. We seemed like grasshoppers in our own eyes, and we looked the same to them."* (Numbers 13:31-33). The report immediately stirred up great fear in the minds of the Israelite people, and they began to grumble against Moses.

The men who scouted the Promised Land and some members of the Israelite assembly witnessed with their very own eyes the miracles that God did for them (e.g., the parting of the Red Sea [Exodus 14:21-22], the turning of bitter water into sweet water [Exodus 15:23-25], and the providing of manna as food [Exodus 16:12-16, 31]) as they came out of Egyptian slavery. No matter what circumstances the Israelites were in, God came through for them every single time. Yet, when they heard the report, the vast majority of the people exhibited fear and did not believe they could have the land of Canaan. Why? Because Satan was manipulating the minds of ten of those twelve men as well as the Israelite assembly.

The reason fear fell upon them was because the people were operating in the flesh, not the Spirit. The ten men who spied on Canaan saw the fortified cities and people already living there with their fleshly eyes, and the Israelite community heard the report from these men with fleshly ears. It is no wonder the Evil One was able to easily inject fear into the hearts of these people. The fear in these people canceled their faith in God and blocked them from seeing that they had already won and received Canaan just as God had promised. The ten men and those Israelites who saw all of God's great miracles in Egypt and the wilderness and were still overtaken by fear and disbelief never saw or entered the Promised Land (Numbers 14:22-23, 29-30, 36-37).

The fear that gripped the Israelites in this story is the same fear that takes hold of investors and those who shy away from stock investing because of stock crashes. But here's what we need to understand: The U.S. stock market has been around since 1792. Since that time, there have been numerous stock market crashes. Three of the worst crashes in U.S. history were the stock market crashes of 1929, 2000, and 2008. Despite all the stock crashes and even the Great Depression of 1933, the U.S. stock market has persevered and continued to march higher over time, erasing every single crash in its entire history to date. Why? Because we have people like Caleb and Joshua, who operate in the Spirit and truth, in our financial system. But even greater, the hands of God are over our financial system, our nation, and the Earth—that is why we cannot and will not be defeated by the Enemy despite him being the prince of the air and the ruler of this world.

It is not a coincidence that the U.S. stock market has continued to thrive since its inception. Although fear, deceptions, and lies from the Enemy fuel stock market crashes, they are no match for the light and the truths of God that always prevail—that is why we are here today and why the U.S. stock market continues to propel to new heights.

Like the Israelites who witnessed firsthand the miracles of God and were still filled with fear, all stock investors, including Christian stock investors, have seen the light and the truths of God work to move the stock market to new heights after every crash. Yet, there is still fear of stock crashes because of some investors and the news media's fleshly perceptions of stock crashes and how they pass on information to the public. However, as children of the one true God, we must always remember that *"God hath not given us the spirit of fear; but of power, and of love, and of sound mind"* (2 Timothy 1:7 KJV). This Spirit of power, love, and sound mind that God has given to us is the Holy Spirit—the Spirit of Truth, who dwells within us. *"...Because the one who is in [us] is greater than the one [Satan] who is in the world"* (1 John 4:4), fear is not in us.

Therefore, we are not going to let stock crashes deter us from wisely investing the money the Lord entrusted to each of us. We are not going to be like the Israelites who were overtaken by fear because of the report they were given about the Promised Land, nor are we going to be like the servant who was given the one talent by his master and hid it in the ground. Instead, we are going to be like Caleb, Joshua, and the two servants who invested and doubled their talents—we must honor and glorify Him who created us in His image. Romans 8:28 tells us, *"...That in all things God works for the good of those who love him, who have been called according to his purpose."* When we invest in the stock market, we are not putting our faith in ourselves or in the world's system. We are placing our faith in God the Almighty that He will see us through and prosper us because we have been called according to His purpose.

Operating in the Spirit is the Key to Surviving Stock Crashes

Since we live in a fallen world, there will always be stock volatility and stock crashes. This is just an inevitable part of stock investing. Despite this, God has shown us over and over again that His hands are over our financial system and the planet. Because of the occasional drops in the market as well as stock crashes, only money that is in savings and will not be touched for ten or more years can be invested. Any money that is needed for living expenses, such as money for mortgage or rent, groceries, utilities, insurance, debts, and so forth, is never to be invested. If you are not sure if you will need the money or not, it's best not to invest it. The long time frame is crucial for two reasons: It allows ample time for our money to grow, and the long time horizon can provide the time needed for recovery should a crash arise. It is important to understand that invested money is not emergency money—that is what an emergency fund is for. That's why I said putting together an emergency fund was an absolute must and cannot be skipped.

In Chapter IX, I illustrated God's financial truths using the S&P 500 and examined a time frame of a little over 30 years from January 1993 to June 2023. In that period, there were four stock crashes: 2000, 2008, 2020, and 2022. Despite these crashes, those who stayed invested did not lose a single penny. I want us to understand that it is during stock crashes that fear has the most power over investors' minds. Many investors have lost thousands or even millions because they succumbed to the spirit of fear and sold their stock holdings when the market was down 20% or more. Do not be like one of these investors. During times such as these, the only way to make it out is to operate in the Spirit like Caleb and Joshua. In other words, have faith in God, see things from His perspective, obey His financial truths, and believe that He will deliver victory. Of the twelve men who scouted the Promised Land, only Caleb and Joshua got to enter and live in it because they had faith and saw things from God's perspective—not from their own fleshly point of view.

Remember King Saul? He feared that the Philistines might overtake him and his Israelite troops at Gilgal. Instead of waiting on God (by waiting for Samuel), Saul took matters into his own hands because of fear and offered up the burnt offering to gain the Lord's favor, which was supposed to have been performed by Samuel. From that point on, Saul's kingship was doomed. If Saul was a stock investor in the year 2008 when stocks took a horrific dive and the S&P 500 declined by almost 60% from its most recent highest point, he would have sold off his entire holdings due to fear near the bottom of this crash just to find out in 2013 that had he just waited on God, his investments would have been just fine. All those investors who made it through those crashes between January 1993 and June 2023 operated in the Spirit whether they believed in God or not. If they hadn't, many of them would have been overtaken by fear and sold off their positions for staggering losses. Only by operating in the Spirit can one cancel out the fear of the Enemy.

A very crucial thing to also know about stocks is that companies who are consistently and increasingly profitable and abide by God's truths will have the financial resources to withstand a market downturn should their ability to generate sales become temporarily impacted by whatever triggered the stock crash. In addition, index funds and ETFs that are designed to track a specific index (like the S&P 500) will also be able to weather a big market drop as the funds contain many financially strong companies. This is why it's so important to diversify a stock portfolio. Diversification not only protects an investor against a few stocks in their position going south (which can happen at any time), but it also helps them to weather any stock market decline.

As I said, every stock crash in the entire history of the U.S. stock market has been erased by a subsequent rebound. Not only that, but stocks as a whole continue to march higher and to new levels. Therefore, there is no reason to sell for a loss. No one, except God, knows when a stock crash will come or when stocks will recover once the market enters a crash. Historically, in nominal terms, it can take anywhere from six months to 25 years for the U.S. stock market to fully return to its most recent highest peak. It was the stock crash of 1929 that took 25 years to recover all its losses, which occurred in 1954. Since then, all subsequent crashes to date have taken less than eight years to recover. Now, can a stock crash like 1929 happen again where the value of the stock market dropped 90%? Absolutely. When? No one knows except for God. Because we do live in a fallen world, this is always a possibility. That's why money that is for living expenses can never be invested, and establishing an emergency fund is a must.

So, what do we do when the market is down? *"Wait for the Lord; be strong and take heart and wait for the Lord"* (Psalm 27:14). Do not look at stock crashes as a bad thing. We should look at them as opportunities to buy more shares at a discount—because that's really what stock crashes are to investors who understand the truth of all this.

The End of the Road for Faith-Based Investment Scams

Many churches and thousands of believers for over a hundred years (probably even centuries) have been defrauded by investment scammers. And guess who's the mastermind behind them all? Satan. As I said at the very beginning of this book, money is necessary to carry out the work of God, and the Enemy will do everything he can to rob God's church and Christians of their money. In doing so, the Serpent hinders our ability to spread the gospel of Jesus Christ and His truths to the world. Two most recent examples of faith-based or religious fraud involved three men who pocketed $27 million from churchgoers in an alleged crypto scheme from 2017 to 2019[1] and a son and his father-in-law who targeted members of God's church and brought in $20 million by offering illegitimate and fake investment offerings from 2018 to 2020.[2]

When it comes to investment scams, the products can be almost anything—not just stocks, bonds, and the alternative vehicles I mentioned. The following are some of the most common characteristics of fake or illegitimate investment products. Most of them promised high returns in a short time (e.g., a few months) or less than a year. Recall that the average annualized return of the S&P 500 is 10-11%. Thus, to entice people to get on board, the fraudsters will say that their products can generate returns much higher than the S&P 500. It's not unheard of for scammers to say that their investments can produce 70% or more in one year or every year. While it is possible for an investment to produce a return greater than 10% in a short period, such a return is difficult to capture and is hard to consistently reproduce. Remember, the real value of an investment is created by work as I previously discussed. Most scam investments do not have this work behind them.

On top of that, most financial products offered by fraudsters are not registered with the SEC or state regulators. Therefore, any investment instrument not registered should be avoided. Now, U.S. government and municipal debts or bonds are exempt from registration, as they are assumed to be safe by regulators. In addition, there are specific investments or securities (e.g., private equity, venture capital, and hedge fund) that are geared toward accredited and high-net-worth investors that are not subject to registration as well. Regardless, always verify the registration and legitimacy of an investment product by checking with the SEC or state securities agency. Of course, since we live in a fallen world, registration doesn't mean that the product is 100% fraud-proof. But knowing this information will help to reduce the chance of fraud.

Despite stock mutual funds, index funds, and ETFs being registered with the SEC, any stock fund could still be a fraud. Why? Because the funds are run by financial institutions, which are themselves run by people with fleshly desires. Therefore, an investment portfolio must hold multiple stock funds, not just one.

Another big thing about scams is that there is a lack of transparency in the way they advertise. Scammers will evade questions that probe the legitimacy of their products. Furthermore, there is a lack of information provided about the investments for investors to make informed decisions. Moreover, many investment offerings are too complex for the average investor to understand. The idea of the Enemy here is to keep investors in the dark as much as possible. Alternative investments can be a breeding ground for fraud because they exhibit these characteristics, which are all countered to God's nature.

But why do churches and individuals of faith fall for such scams? Scammers prey on faith organizations and believers by using their faith against them. In many cases, the fraudsters are Christians themselves or pose as genuine believers. In other scenarios, the people doing the scamming simply build enough trust with the folks they intend to defraud. Furthermore, anyone can be an investment scammer—a friend, family member, spouse, colleague, stranger, or believer. Scripture makes it very clear in Romans 3:10 and 12 that *"There is no one righteous, not even one. All have turned away...."* Further, Romans 3:23 says, *"...All have sinned and fall short of the glory of God."* It may be difficult to digest the fact that Christians can defraud or betray other Christians. However, this shouldn't be a surprise. Judas Iscariot was one of Jesus's twelve disciples and a close friend. Yet, it was he who betrayed Christ and turned Him over to the Jewish religious leaders.

In addition to the fact that investment scammers disguise themselves as followers of the Lord to deceive His children, our flesh provides the Enemy with two more advantages (after all, our flesh is an ally of the Serpent). What are these advantages? The flesh loves money and rejects knowledge and wisdom (which I previously mentioned in Chapter V). This is why God wanted to include the account of Judas Iscariot in the Bible for our example—because he loved money and rejected knowledge and wisdom (since his mind was ruled by his flesh).

Since Judas loved money, Satan was able to exploit that desire with his lies to cause Judas to betray Jesus for 30 pieces of silver. As of early December 2023, the price of silver was approximately $25 per ounce, and 30 pieces of silver (based on the Tyrian shekels of silver coin) weighed about 13 ounces. Thus, Christ was sold out for = ($25 x 13) = $325. For comparison, in Chapter III, Delilah handed over Samson to the Philistines for $53,350. The love of money is a heart issue and not about the amount involved or whether a person is rich or poor. Abraham was extremely wealthy, but he did not love money. The young rich ruler from Matthew 19:16-22, on the other hand, was rich and loved money and things.

Not only that, but Judas does not seek financial knowledge and wisdom. Thus, the Devil was able to persuade Judas to continually steal money from Jesus's ministry. Also, because of his lack of financial wisdom, Judas never made a counteroffer when the Jewish priests offered him 30 pieces of silver for betraying Jesus, which only affirms his financial ignorance.

Why didn't Judas just ask Jesus to teach him how to best build wealth? After all, the guy was with the Messiah—the

Creator of everything—for three years! Jesus could have taught Judas how to become the wealthiest person to have ever lived had he just humbly asked Him and done what was right. Instead, he resorted to stealing from and betraying the Lord.

In all cases of investment scams, it is the love/want of money and lack of financial knowledge and wisdom that enables the Enemy to deceive individuals. The Serpent can't deceive a person in something they don't love/want or know is not true. For example, in Genesis 39:7-10, Potiphar's wife tried to persuade Joseph to go to bed with her daily. But Joseph refused her because that was something he did not want since his mind was set on God, not his flesh. In Acts 5:1-4, Ananias tried to deceive Peter about the money he brought to the apostles after selling off his land. However, since Peter was given a word of knowledge from God, Ananias could not trick Peter into believing that the money brought to them was all of the proceeds from the sale of his land as Ananias made it out to be. This principle also applies to situations of investment scams as well. If an individual does not love/want money, they cannot be deceived by such scams. Or if a person knows the truth about an investment—that it is fake or exhibits characteristics of an investment scam as discussed—they cannot be deceived as well.

So, how can churches and Christians avoid or greatly minimize the chance of investment scams? *"Get [financial] wisdom, get [financial] understanding"* (Proverbs 4:5). Satan, the Great Deceiver, knows that financial knowledge and wisdom are the keys to stopping him from financially defrauding God's church and His children. That is why Satan has been working so hard to keep us from realizing this truth. For the Enemy knows that when we "...*know the truth...the truth will set [us] free*" (John 8:32). Together, we can stop the Enemy from robbing us as individual believers and God's church. The one who created us has given us the power via the Holy Spirit and His truths to completely derail the Devil's efforts to continue to steal from us and thwart our work to bring all people to know Him!

The financial field is vast and continuously evolving. New investment products are constantly being introduced into the financial markets. Because of this, the Enemy is always looking for a gap in our financial knowledge and wisdom to deceive us. Just because he cannot deceive us now doesn't mean the Devil will ever stop trying to destroy us financially. This is why Ecclesiastes 7:12 tells us, "*Wisdom is a shelter as money is a shelter, but the advantage of knowledge is this: Wisdom preserves those who have it.*" Therefore, we must never stop learning, and we must educate ourselves on all financial and investment products that are in the different financial markets. Not only that, but we must be prudent and do research on every investment offer that comes our way.

Until Jesus Christ comes back to Earth and puts the Serpent in his place permanently, he will never cease to "*...steal and kill and destroy*" (John 10:10). Thus, we must "*be alert and of sober mind. [For the] enemy the devil prowls around like a roaring lion looking for someone to devour*" (1 Peter 5:8). To always be in a spiritual state of financial alertness, we must put God's financial truths into action in our financial life.

Investing in God's Kingdom Is a Win for All of Humanity

When a person invests in the kingdom of God, everyone (including that person) wins. For example, the Pharaoh of Egypt during Joseph's time was very wise and knew very well the financial and economic consequences of not heeding the words of Joseph concerning his dreams. That was why he said to the young Hebrew man: *"Since God has made all this [the famine] known to you, there is no one so discerning and wise as you. You shall be in charge of my palace, and all my people are to submit to your orders"* (Genesis 41:39-40). By making Joseph his deputy and putting him in charge of the efforts to avert a potentially catastrophic impact from the coming famine, Pharaoh was investing in the kingdom of God. In doing so, the investment paid off for Pharaoh and his people in the sense that the Egyptians and their country were saved.

Not only that, but the decision of Pharaoh to put Joseph in charge made the world of that time better off, too. It did so by making Egypt the economic and supply powerhouse when the famine finally came upon the lands. During this time, all the people came to buy from Egypt. Furthermore, Pharaoh's decision to invest in God's kingdom benefited all of humanity for all times, including ours today. The action that Pharaoh took paved the way for Jesus Christ to come into the world to save mankind from sin, fully redeem us, and reestablish the connection between God and humanity that was severed by the Enemy after he tricked Adam and Eve into eating from the Tree of Knowledge. Even though the Egyptians had their gods

(Exodus 12:12), Pharaoh and his people were still willing to partner with the kingdom of God.

When I say invest in God's kingdom, I am not talking about money (although this seems to be what many people, including Christians, have in mind when there is talk of sowing into God's church). God isn't interested in our money because it already belongs to Him. What I am referring to is the willingness and obedience of a person, which is exactly what God looks for and is far more important to Him than any amount of money. This is analogous to what Samuel said to King Saul about sacrifice and obedience. After Saul failed to completely wipe out the Amalekites as God commanded, Samuel said to him: *"Does the Lord delight in burnt offerings and sacrifices as much as in obeying the Lord? To obey is better than sacrifice..."* (1 Samuel 15:22). God is far more interested in our willingness and obedience than our money. A ministry can have all the money in the world, but without willingness and obedience, the money can do nothing.

Joseph, too, was investing in the kingdom of God by being willing and obedient to the Lord. For this, he was elevated by God through Pharaoh to become the second most powerful person in Egypt. Joseph's ascension to the office of prime minister of Egypt fulfilled the prophecy of his dreams (when he was a young boy) that he would rule over his brothers and family. In addition, Joseph's willingness and obedience played a significant part in the Israelites' return to the Promised Land and ultimately to the coming of Christ through the House of David to bless all people, just as God had initially promised Abraham.

Our God is no respecter of persons as Peter finally understood in Acts 10:34-35 when he spoke to the Gentiles at Cornelius's house. To them, he said, *"I have now realized how true it is that God does not show favoritism but accepts from every nation the one who fears him and does what is right."* God will accept anyone willing and obedient to carry out His plans regardless of whether they are a somebody like Pharaoh or a nobody like Joseph (before he was promoted), a believer or unbeliever, circumcised or uncircumcised, rich or poor, educated or uneducated, and so on. One time, John told Jesus that he and the disciples saw a person casting out demons in the name of Jesus, and the disciples told the individual to stop because he was not one of them. However, in response, Jesus said to the disciples: *"Do not stop him... For no one who does a miracle in my name can in the next moment say anything bad about me, for whoever is not against us is for us"* (Mark 9:39-40). Therefore, we, too, must not be a respecter of persons. We should accept anyone who fears the Lord, wants to partner with God's kingdom, and/or desires to further His work here on the planet.

In Matthew 28:19-20, Jesus said to his disciples: *"... Go and make disciples of all nations, baptizing them in the name of the Father and of the Son and of the Holy Spirit, and teaching them to obey everything I have commanded you."* When Peter, John, and the other disciples willingly carried out this commandment, they, too, were all investing in the kingdom of God. Because of their willingness and obedience to spread the good news of Jesus Christ, God was able to build up these disciples—who were once confused, scared, and weak-minded—into incredibly strong spiritual believers with no fear of anything in this world. Not even death could stop them from teaching and preaching the Word of God.

Even more important, we get to benefit from their investments. As Christians today, we have eternal salvation and are the sons and daughters of the God most high. In addition, we have the power through the Holy Spirit to heal the sick, cast out evil spirits, and perform miracles. We also have the Bible to help us be successful in every area of life, including our finances. All of these benefits were only made available to us because of the decision, willingness, and obedience of the disciples and those who came before us who invested in the Lord's kingdom.

My fellow brothers and sisters in Christ, when Satan deceived Adam and Eve and caused them to eat from the Tree of Knowledge, that was the day that he launched a full-scale spiritual assault on mankind. Because of the Enemy's spiritual influences and attacks, this world has experienced much destruction and suffering. The Devil's spiritual warfare against humanity encompasses many battles as I said at the beginning of this book. One such battle that we all must fight (whether we want to or not) is the spiritual battle for our financial health. Jesus Christ came to Earth to bring us love, joy, wisdom, and victory. And God gave us free will to turn away from Satan's deceit and away from financial difficulty.

So, what am I saying here? I am saying that we have a choice. We can end the spiritual fight for our financial health and claim victory in our finances today because God has already made the financial knowledge and wisdom available to us in the Bible as well as in this book. Even better, we can end this entire war altogether and have victory in every area of our lives. How? By investing in the kingdom of God—that is, by taking up the sword of the Spirit and put on the full armor of God. In doing so, we signify that we are willing and obedient to the Word. In other words, what we are doing by being willing and obedient is ceding our will in exchange for God's will to be done. In doing so, victory permeates through every area of our life (not just our finances). The Enemy and his army of fallen angels flee in great terror when Christians unite and each draws the sword of the Spirit from their pouches for battle against them.

It is not in the will of God that any should perish (2 Peter 3:9). Financial difficulty in our own life will not keep us out of Heaven if we are saved, but it may keep others out because we were unable to reach them with the Lord's truths. Therefore, the decision that we make today to invest in His kingdom will not only bring victory to our finances, enable us to be a financial blessing to others, and allow us to live the financial life that God intends for us, but our collective financial victory in the body of Christ will enable us to greatly channel God's truths to all of humanity. As we spread the Word of God to all corners of the globe, leaving no stone unturned, we are helping to save souls, bring Heaven to Earth, and transform lives for the betterment of all mankind as we all wait for the second coming of the Lord Jesus Christ.

Isaiah 1:19 says, *"If you are willing and obedient, you will eat the good things of the land."* As Christians, when we invest in the kingdom of God not only do we reap the harvest but so does the entire world—and it's all for His glory!

References:

[1] Malwa, S. (2020, August 29). Scammers Pose as Religious Workers in $27 Million Crypto Fraud, Alleges SEC. Decrypt. https://decrypt.co/40148/scammers-pose-as-religious-workers-in-27-million-crypto-fraud-alleges-sec

[2] SEC Alleges Son and Father-in-Law Touted Faith to Target Church Members in $20 Million Offering Fraud. (2023, May 2). US Securities and Exchange Commission. https://www.sec.gov/news/press-release/2023-84

ABOUT THE AUTHOR

Ken has accepted Jesus Christ as his Lord and Savior since 2012. In Joshua 1:8 God told Joshua the son of Nun: *"Keep this Book of the Law [which today is the Bible] always on your lips; meditate on it day and night, so that you may be careful to do everything written in it. Then you will be prosperous and successful."* That's why Ken firmly believes that the Word of God is the key to success in every area of life. However, to experience success according to God's truths—that is to eat the good things of the land, one must be willing and obedient (Isaiah 1:19).

As a follower of the one true God, Ken wholeheartedly agrees with what the Apostle Paul said in 1 Corinthians 12:12-27 concerning the truth that every believer is a part of one body—that is the Body of Christ. As such, every Christian has an important role to fill and work to do in the ministry of Jesus Christ to bring all people to know the truth of God. Thus, one of Ken's ministry callings from God is to help build up every believer so that each becomes willing and obedient to the Word. In this way, they can tap into and use their God-given gifts to serve in whatever ministry area they have been called to.

It was God who enabled Ken to discover and develop his gift in the areas of finance and investing. Ken has a strong understanding of the Scripture (God's financial truths) and its application to personal finance as well as over a decade of experience and success trading and investing in the stock market. In addition, he has a strong background in statistics and probability and their applications to investing. Further, Ken possesses a deep knowledge and understanding of various financial and investment products, which include:

- Stocks, bonds, mutual funds, exchange-traded funds (ETFs), and money markets
- Initial public offerings (IPOs), private equities, venture capitals, hedge funds, and securitized investment products
- Real estate investment trusts (REITs), forex, commodities, and crypto currencies
- Nonfungible tokens (NFTs), options trading, futures market, foreign and emerging markets, and inverse and leverage funds

Moreover, Ken holds an Associate of Applied Science from the Community College of the U.S. Air Force and Bachelor of Science and Master of Science degrees from the University of Massachusetts Lowell. As of this book's publication, Ken is studying the Word of God at Rhema Bible Training College (RBTC) with a focus in Itinerant Ministry.

ABOUT KENTON LOR MINISTRIES

Ken is the founder of Kenton Lor Ministries, an anointed and gifted teacher of the Word of God, and a servant of the God Most High. The Lord desires that every believer live a life of excellence, holiness, and success reflective of Him who created us and for His glory. Therefore, Ken's ministry is focused not only on teaching God's truths but also on the application of the Word in a person's life so that they may be set free (John 8:32) and live a life of abundance (John 10:10). Founded on the premise of Isaiah 1:19, Kenton Lor Ministries operates four unique ministerial arms as follow:

- *imitating HIM (General Ministry)*
  To train believers to be like Jesus or be doers of the Word through faith and help them to discover and use their God-given gifts to serve the kingdom of God and others.
- *Financial Victory. God'$ Way! (Financial Ministry)*
  To educate God's children on His financial truths so they can be good financial stewards and live the financial life the Lord intends for them.

- *Choose God Over Drugs (Toxicology Ministry)*
  To educate believers on the truths and dangers of drugs and equip them with the Word so that they choose God over drug abuse and overdose.
- *Show Me the Father IN HIM (Fatherhood Ministry)*
  To impart God's fatherly truths to born again Christian men and train them to become the fathers that God intends for them to be.

To learn more about Kenton Lor Ministries or to invite Ken to speak/teach, please:
- Visit our website at www.kentonlorministries.org
- Contact us via email at truth@kentonlorministries.org

You may also inquire more about Kenton Lor Ministries by writing to us at:

Kenton Lor Ministries
P.O. Box 150264
Tulsa, OK 74115

TO THE READER

On behalf of Kenton Lor Ministries, I want to thank you very much for your purchase and support of this book. All the proceeds from the sales of this book (for as long as the book is in circulation) will go towards supporting other ministries, such as missions, churches, outreaches, Bible training, and so forth, in the kingdom of God. Your purchase of this book is helping to move forward God's kingdom as well as bring more people to know the truth, love, and abundant life of the Lord.

I strongly believe that God's financial truths contained within this book will be a great blessing to you, your family, and everyone that you share this book or its information with as it did for me and my family.

Again, thank you and God bless you.

www.ingramcontent.com/pod-product-compliance
Lightning Source LLC
Chambersburg PA
CBHW070057080526
44586CB00013B/1102